Parenting children

for a life of faith

Helping children meet and know God

Rachel Turner

For my parents, Terry and Susan Hart, whose quiet sacrifice, unending love and good-natured determination have daily rooted me in the knowledge and experience of God. I will never know all that you did for me, but I am so blessed to reap the fruit of it in my life. Thank you.

Acknowledgments

Sue Doggett, thank you for finding me and believing in me enough to insist on us going on this journey together. You have set me on this book writing path and have given me grace at every turn.

Helen Shannon and New Wine, you challenged me to take a close look at connecting children to God's heart and gave me a venue in which to play. I wouldn't be here without the space you carved out for me.

St Paul's Church, St Albans family, you welcomed me with open arms, loved me and let me grow and experiment in how to minister. You greeted every new idea with enthusiasm and allowed me the honour of being involved in your lives. This book is our learning curve together.

My three wise women—Lesley Kempsford, Anne Garside and Heather Mack—you have guided me when I was lost, held me up when I had no strength, given me hope when I had none and have never flagged in your encouragement or support. Thank you.

Liz Baddaley and Jill Andrews, thank you for sharing life with me and loving me enough to read endless versions of these chapters. I am blessed to have friends with such selflessness and skill.

Jo and Elliot Ireton and James and Susie Yeates, you have kept me fired up and on course. We are so blessed to have you as partners in ministry.

Mom and Dad, Mom for lending your talents to this book and keeping me laughing all the way through it; Dad for never letting me get off the phone without praying for me.

Mark, my husband, you have walked every step of the way with me on this journey. Thank you for never letting me give up, for empowering and supporting me day after day, and for your seemingly endless well of grace, love, joy, and sacrifice. We have birthed this together!

Rachel Turner is currently the Family Life Pastor at St Paul's Church, Hammersmith. She has been a full-time children's worker in churches around the UK, and the National Children's Work Coordinator for New Wine. She continues to consult, speak at conferences and run training days for parents, children and youth workers around the UK and Europe. Her work has brought her into contact with thousands of children and families through mainstream New Wine summer events, parish weekends, schools and daily encounters in her own church. Through her work, Rachel has developed significant and transforming opportunities to introduce children into a loving, lasting relationship with God, based on her experience of connecting to God through prayer and nurturing a lifelong journey of faith. She has also written Parenting Children for a Life of Purpose (BRF, 2014) and Parenting Children for a Life of Confidence (BRF, 2015).

Text copyright © Rachel Turner 2010
The author asserts the moral right
to be identified as the author of this work

Published by
The Bible Reading Fellowship
15 The Chambers, Vineyard
Abingdon OX14 3FE
United Kingdom
Tel: +44 (0)1865 319700
Email: enquiries@brf.org.uk
Website: www.brf.org.uk
BRF is a Registered Charity

ISBN 978 1 84101 607 8

First published 2010
Reprinted 2012, 2013, 2015
10 9 8 7 6 5 4 3
All rights reserved

Acknowledgements
Unless otherwise stated, scripture quotations are taken from the Contemporary English
Version of the Bible published by HarperCollins Publishers, copyright © 1991, 1992, 1995
American Bible Society.

Scripture quotations taken from the Holy Bible, New International Version, copyright © 1973,
1978, 1984 by International Bible Society, are used by permission of Hodder & Stoughton
Publishers, a division of Hodder Headline Ltd. All rights reserved. 'NIV' is a registered
trademark of International Bible Society. UK trademark number 1448790.

Cover image: © Getty images/Flickr

Every effort has been made to trace and contact copyright owners for material used in this
resource. We apologise for any inadvertent omissions or errors, and would ask those concerned
to contact us so that full acknowledgement can be made in the future.

A catalogue record for this book is available from the British Library

Printed by CPI Group (UK) Ltd, Croydon CR0 4YY

Contents

*

Foreword

Rachel had me hooked by the third line of her book. Like many mums with sport-loving sons, I've experienced the longings she describes in her introduction. Most Christian parents long for their children to enjoy a deeper relationship with God—a relationship that is real and relevant to every aspect of their lives. We long to give our children strong spiritual foundations, which can equip them to become mature Christian adults. Sadly, we all know children who have grown up in loving families and great churches, but have never connected with God on a personal level.

Rachel's analysis of the problem is inspired: by highlighting the difference between 'God-smart' and 'God-connected' children, she points to the heart of the issue—and to some steps parents can take to make a difference. By using real stories, she helps bring theory to life, showing us how to help our children hold on to biblical truth, while experiencing a growing relationship with God.

Not all Christian parents will have the opportunity to put Rachel's suggestions into practice from the beginning of their parenting years. Not everyone will have the support of a like-minded husband or wife. Not all parents will have experienced God in the ways Rachel describes. Don't panic! As a result of reading Rachel's book, all Christian parents will be challenged and encouraged to develop a deeper relationship with God themselves and to create windows into that experience, so that their children see how they, too, can live connected to God.

Catherine Butcher
Former Editor, Families First *magazine*

*

Introduction

'I just don't know what to do any more.' Sarah's face twisted in frustration and exhaustion as she shared her heart with me. Like many mums, she desperately longed for her son to enjoy church and have some sort of input about God. Lately, they had been heatedly clashing about Chris' desire to play football on a Sunday instead of attending church. 'He's eleven years old, and I still don't know if God is real to him at all.' She sighed deeply. 'I don't even know if he's really a Christian. What did I do wrong?'

Jemma had recently come into a relationship with God through an Alpha course and had been bringing her four-year-old daughter Jasmine to church ever since. She had seen that Jasmine didn't understand the changes that had been happening in their lives as a result of her decision, but she knew that her daughter had noticed a difference. Jemma was unsure how to talk about her faith with her child, much less how to help Jasmine have an experience with God herself. She longed for Jasmine to have a life with him in the way that she did and was determined to give her daughter a childhood full of faith, but had no idea where to start, or how to include her unbelieving partner on the journey.

Richard and Jill have three children. Lily, their middle child, is an eight-year-old girl with big brown eyes, a cheeky, toothy grin, and floppy brown hair. She often had to arrive early to church as her parents helped out on the PA and coffee rotas and with the children's groups. Raised in a Christian two-parent home, Lily had been part of the church world since she was born. She knew the right answers to almost every question in Sunday school, which made her feel very clever indeed. Children at school bullied her a lot, and often her afternoons featured either a crying fit or an angry outburst at her sister, followed by an extended time in her room, sulking and upset. All the right answers from church couldn't help her work out why she felt the way she did, and how to stop the words that kept going around in her head. All the phrases played as she got ready in the morning and lay down at night: 'stupid', 'ugly', 'why don't you just go and die?' and 'useless' echoed endlessly. She felt that she was a disappointment to God and to her parents. Richard and Jill seemed at a loss as to how to stop this slow slide in their daughter's confidence. Every night when they put their daughter to bed, they tried to make it a habit to pray. Lily rarely prayed out loud, most of the time preferring Richard or Jill to say her prayers for her. They tried to keep it simple—asking Lily what she wanted to say 'sorry' and 'thank you' for, and what she wanted to ask for from God. They knew that Lily was a 'Christian' but their hearts ached, wishing their daughter was able to find the peace, vibrancy and power that they found in their own faith.

We instinctively know that there is a difference between a child who knows about God and a child whose heart and life are connected to him. When we know in our own lives the transformational power and daily sustenance of a heart in connection with God, we want our children to benefit from a similar relationship. Somehow, though, we only get as far as building God-smart children, hoping that eventually, somehow, God-smart will turn into God-connected. In most cases, this isn't reality. Knowing about God is important but, if we work only on developing knowledge, we are robbing our children of what they were designed for—to be in relationship with God.

As a children's minister at a church, I hear people's stories over and over again: different stories, different circumstances, but the same uneasy, questioning look in their eyes. They feel that their children are missing something vital in their lives and are struggling with how to resolve it. It doesn't seem to matter whether they are single parents, divorced or married couples, people who are new to the faith or those who have been raised in it. Some people have brand new babies, some children or teenagers, and some are struggling with how to help their grown-up children. They want more for their children spiritually than what they already have. They want all that God has for them, now and in the future, but it all feels so hard.

In my work, I am continually struck by how disempowered parents feel about their role in the spiritual direction and lives of their children. No matter how many parents I speak to, in churches and communities all over the UK, a theme resonates. 'I want my children to meet and know God—to live a vibrant life with him! But how do I get them there?'

Some people feel that the answer is the church, 'The church must do more, do better, do something.' Money and effort are poured into Sunday programmes, holiday clubs and midweek groups. In some cases, this effort produces fruit. Children do grow in their knowledge of God, though some love church and others don't. The problem is that, in most cases, it doesn't result in God-connected children, just God-smart ones. People want more for their children; church is seemingly unable to provide it, and so the frustration grows.

Some people turn to resources such as Bible reading notes to fill the spiritual void. They plan 'family time' nights when they read the Bible and study it together. They read Bible notes in the mornings together over breakfast, fill the house with Christian DVDs, read great Christian children's books, and play under-fives' worship CDs until they want to scream. In many cases, it produces fruit. Children grow in their knowledge of God and the right answers to spiritual questions. Yet, in most cases, it still doesn't result in God-connected children, just God-smart ones. People want more for their children, and resources alone are unable to provide it.

There seem to be mountains of parenting books detailing good methods of developing Christian morals, discipline, encouragement, worldview and education. This book is not one of those. This book is about how to help guide a child to meet and know God in a vibrant way in his or her everyday life. It is about how to parent our children into a reality of God's presence and love, to equip them to access him themselves, and to train them how to build and grow in a two-way relationship with him that will last a lifetime. It aims to equip us to empower our children to be God-connected as well as God-smart.

My goal in writing this book is to empower parents and prime carers to be filled with confidence in their ability to proactively and transparently guide their children to a life-giving relationship with God. All the stories in this book are true, either taken from my own experiences or reported to me by parents who have been involved in them—only the names have been changed. The more real stories we hear, the more encouraged we can become. Included in the book are suggested questions to consider as we go on this journey together.

God has chosen us to raise our children to meet and know him, and to live with him every day through to eternity. He has already been equipping and training us to do this job well. I pray that this book will empower each one of us to embrace our role and take the next step on our journey of parenting.

*

Part One

Positioning for influence

I was sitting in the back of a large seminar room on a very uncomfortable hard cushioned seat. The seminar speaker was chattering on about all-age services and I had let my mind wander. Then a question from a man in the audience brought me back into the room with a thump. 'What about us parents? Shouldn't the church be helping us do faith at home?' I shifted in my seat to see what the speaker would say. With a smile, she breezily replied, 'I just encourage the parents in my church to be Jesus to their children, so, as their children see them, they will see God.' Wham! There you go, parents—no pressure. Be Jesus. Your child's spiritual development depends on it. The man's face flickered, half smiling as he sat back down. His shoulders slumped a bit. He glanced sideways at his wife holding their baby and she smiled weakly back.

I left the seminar room feeling frustrated. Of course we should all strive to be more Christ-like in our lives, but if my child's connection to God is based on my perfect expression of Jesus, then he doesn't have a chance. No child does. I'm a failure before I even begin. Is God's design really that we should 'be Jesus', living the perfect life in front of our children, so that they see him in us and therefore know him through us? We all hope that we do radiate Christ[1] and therefore share part of his wonderful nature with our children. But is that the primary way in which our children are to meet and experience him? Is that the design? I don't think so. I believe that God chooses us as parents and prime carers to be the primary spiritual influencers in our children's lives, and to do three main things: to disciple and mentor our children proactively in their relationship with God, to model the reality of what a real relationship with God looks like close up, and to help children to tie together biblical truth and their experiences of life and of God.

Note
1.   2 Corinthians 3:18

*

— Chapter 1 —

Discipling proactively

Marnie looked around the seminar room uncertainly as she began to describe her childhood for the other parents in my class. She grew up in a very strict Christian home. 'My parents forced religion down our throats whether we liked it or not.' Her parents demanded a lot of spiritual performance from her and her siblings as they grew up. 'God seemed like an angry man who was watching our every move. It felt like he was just waiting for us to sin so he could pour out his wrath on to our little lives.' She fumbled with a tissue in her hands as she explained her teenage rebellion against her parents and against the religion that, she felt, ruled her life. Her journey took her far away and, when she finally hit rock bottom, she discovered God for who he really is. For the first time, she built a relationship with God and saw it change her life. She now wants her children to experience the same connection that she feels with God, but she is afraid. 'When I look at my children, I see that they are not "God connected". To be honest, I was so afraid of repeating how my parents spiritually brought me up that I have tried to take a back seat completely. I want my children to choose a faith for themselves, not because I forced it on them but because they want it. I want them to go at their pace and have it be completely their choice.' She sighed. 'The problem is that their pace is non-existent. I just don't see any desire within them to know God. I don't know what to do.'

Passive/reactive influencing

Many of us struggle to balance our desires in this area. On the one hand, we want to get strongly involved with our children's spiritual development. On the other, we want our children to choose faith of their own accord, so that they don't end up pushing God away in an attempt at independence from us.

Many of us are content to get on with our own relationship with God but have a fear of 'crossing the line' too far with our children and accidentally driving them away. This can lead to a very reactive style of spiritual parenting. We wait, hanging on for magical 'teachable moments' to come along: a crisis at school, a random spiritual question from our wayward pre-teenagers, a family emergency or other large event when we see a flicker of spiritual openness in our child. When this glimmer appears, we try to cram every piece of spiritual information, theology and practical biblical application into the opportunity we get, because who knows when the chance will arise again?

It's a little like playing in a group with a skipping rope in the playground. Generally, there are some unspoken rules of the game: the skipper must do tricks, skip on one leg, take no more than 30 seconds—however the group playground rules have evolved. The person waiting has to figure out the pace and rope position, successfully jump inside the death trap of the circling rope, jump a few times over the rope as it passes beneath her feet, and manage to jump out again without damaging herself or the rope's path. If she fails, it all comes crumbling down: the rope's journey is over and everyone shakes their head in disappointment. She has to wait at the back of the queue for another turn.

Many of us feel this way about spiritually influencing our children. We need to find an opportunity presented by our child, figure out the 'rules' of that interaction, avoid all the obstacles and the swinging defensiveness of the child, get in, do our thing, get out again without messing up and causing upset to our child or rebellion against God, and emerge on the other side victorious with a successful conversation about God (and some potential action points that may or may not be followed up). Hurrah! We then walk around as if we are ten feet tall. Behold—the spiritually influencing parent. If it goes badly, though, we feel crushed. We may feel as if we've hurt our child's view of God or Christianity, and we fear that it will be a long time until he or she gives us an opportunity like that again.

This style of reactive parenting seems to be unique to the spiritual aspects of the parent–child relationship. I can't recall many parents I've met saying, 'I don't want my child to feel like he *must* go to school. I want him to choose it out of his own desire for intellectual growth and stimulation'; or, 'Brushing teeth and washing are optional in our house. I never want my children to feel *forced* into personal hygiene. I want them to choose it for themselves'; or, 'I don't want my child to be *pushed* into having friends. Clearly, she prefers crying in a corner by herself. If I get involved, she may rebel against having friends altogether.' Certain aspects of our children's lives, we know, are important for us to care about and be involved in. We know that our influence is essential to give our children a safe, prosperous life, and so we wade in. But for some reason, our children's spiritual health and happiness often don't receive the same careful attention.

Proactive discipling

God desires us to be proactive with our children's upbringing, including their spiritual development. We are designed to influence our children's mental, emotional, physical and spiritual growth— and we need not feel intimidated or ashamed that spiritual growth is part of that list.

Passing on spiritual values doesn't happen casually. If a person has a wonderful and full faith, this doesn't mean that it will automatically trickle into his or her child. We can see this over and over again in the Bible. Many great spiritual pillars in the Bible were passive spiritual parents and reaped the consequences. Jacob, forefather of the twelve tribes of Israel, was so passive that when some of his children slaughtered all the men in a town, or sold their brother into slavery, or committed incest, he did nothing.[1] His passivity allowed for his children to grow up virtually unaware of God's call. King David also refused to step in when his son raped his own half-sister and was then killed by her brother.[2] This 'man after God's own heart',[3] this wonderful servant of God, struggled to pass on to his sons the way to live in relationship with God. Jacob and David had a place of influence in the lives of their children, but they squandered their time and position, and their children's spiritual lives were affected.

God makes his designs clear for our proactive discipleship of our children, very early on in the Bible. In Deuteronomy 6:4–9 we read:

Listen, Israel! The Lord our God is the only true God! So love the Lord your God with all your heart, soul, and strength. Memorise his laws and tell them to your children over and over again. Talk about them all the time, whether you're at home or walking along the road or going to bed at night, or getting up in the morning. Write down copies and tie them to your wrists and foreheads to help you obey them. Write these laws on the door frames of your homes and on your town gates.

This is not a passive spiritual parenting model. God wants his children to be close to him, and he wants us to make the family home the centre of our spiritual discussion and relationship with him. In both Old and New Testaments, loving God with all our heart, soul, mind and strength is the goal of this spiritual training. God is calling us actively to create a life of spiritual influence for our children that pervades their everyday world.

If we want to influence our children in the everyday, we need to ensure that we are giving ourselves the crucial time required to shape their experiences. God very cleverly designed us so that influence in each other's lives equals time spent together, so he made sure that we parents were the people who had the most time with our children. In today's world, we recognise the busyness of family life but, even so, we still do spend a lot of time with our children. In the morning, after school, in the car, at home, at weekends, on holiday, and through the summer, our children and teenagers can't get away from us. We may not feel that we have a lot of time with them, but God has provided it.

Some of us have allowed busyness to steal away the time God designed for us to have with our children, to influence and share with them. If so, we will need to begin to place a higher value on our spiritual influence in their lives. Positioning ourselves for influence may require some schedule-changing, to carve out more time with our children. Some of us have the time already built into our schedules, but we struggle to see it. It is easy to spot the large chunks of time available: evenings off, lazy Sunday afternoons, holidays, or times when the age-old cry of 'I'm bored' drifts towards our ears. The opportunities that are harder to see are the shorter periods that God gives us: five minutes while making the lunches for school, time spent driving in the car on the way to another sporting event, queuing up at the supermarket, or sitting with one child while waiting for another to finish an activity.

All of these tiny minutes add up into a pattern of involvement in the lives of our children that can be used in powerful ways. We just have to know how to position ourselves so that when we have carved out those times and taken advantage of the moments we are given, we are ready to influence. Positioning for influence is not a question of 'one more thing' to squeeze into our already full days. It is about making the decision to disciple our children proactively and to create and utilise the time to do it well.

Questions for reflection

- What might you need to change in order to position yourself to influence your children spiritually?
- What things do you allow into your life that steal time you could be spending with your children?

- What small chunks of time do you already have in your schedule that you use to disciple your child proactively?

_____

Notes
1. Genesis 34; 37; 38
2. 2 Samuel 13
3. 1 Samuel 13:14 (NIV)

— Chapter 2 —

Modelling the reality of relationship

Nine-year-old Shaun has worked out over the past two years that doing the 'God thing' generally consists of being in a crowd of varying sizes, doing things together for God. At church, they sing together about God, pray together, talk about him together, and do craft together to remember what they have learnt about him. At home, they say grace together at meals, and at bedtime his parents pray with him before he goes to sleep. Sometimes his family read Bible stories together, and they do loads of Christian stuff with church and community at Easter and Christmas. Every once in a while, his family join others from the church in doing practical 'outreach' events like a harvest party or giving out food at a homeless shelter. The confusing part is that everyone talks about having a 'personal relationship' with God, but what does that mean? Sure, God is real and exists, but, from what Shaun has seen, he doesn't have much to do with everyday life, does he?

Shaun is not alone in his questions. Many children fall into a similar pattern of life. It is a huge challenge for them to picture what a relationship with God looks like, because they have honestly never seen it before. In our efforts to 'teach' our children, we have tended primarily to create corporate situations in which to do it. Many times this is for noble reasons: wanting the family to worship together or wanting to be part of a vibrant church life. The problem is that we surround our children with experiences and models of engaging with God in a group, and then expect them to know how to have a vibrant individual relationship with him.

I once worked for a church as a part-time assistant secretary for a youth pastor on a large staff team. The head pastor was a wonderful, godly, humble man whom I greatly respected, but my whole experience of him was from a distance. A couple of times, I was one of 20 staff members in the staff dining room while the pastor talked and laughed and told stories, but I don't think I ever personally spoke during those times. I was part of the thousands-strong congregation as we listened to him speak and as he ministered to us. He prayed for me once, for a couple of seconds, as he worked his way around a group of people who came forward as part of a response during a service. I was very comfortable with my relationship with him as part of the crowd. I knew my place and the level of relationship I could expect as part of the crowd. It was good—until the staff retreat.

Every year, the staff of the church would take a couple of days away to spend time together, get some spiritual input and hear what the senior leadership had planned for the following year. During a break, a few of us secretaries chose to go swimming. As we were arriving back at the hotel, we ran into the senior staff team chatting in the lobby. Inside, I began to panic. This was not your normal crowd/pastor scenario. I stood there, hair in spikes, mascara running down my face, wrapped in a robe and dripping on the lobby carpet, perfectly decent but feeling very vulnerable. I tried to blend into the wall as I watched my head pastor continue to chat and laugh with his colleagues, oblivious to our presence.

Unfortunately, circumstances dictated that there wasn't enough room for me in the lift going up, and so I was left behind to wait for the next available one. It felt as if time slowed to a near stop. As I watched in horror, the senior staff team got up and left the lobby, evidently to retrieve the car, leaving my head pastor behind with the bags. He casually looked around and noticed me, part of his crowd, alone and looking uncomfortable. He wandered over to me to say hello, and shyness overtook me. For six years, I had been part of his crowd, and then suddenly found myself face to face with my leader in an empty lobby.

It was in that moment that I knew I had no idea how to have

a one-to-one conversation with him, at all. I knew so much about him but, in that moment, I just froze. What could I talk about? What should I ask? Does he care to know? Should I crack a joke? Acknowledge my state of appearance? Ignore it? Act casual? Assume he knows me? Introduce myself? I know he is a kind and considerate person—I've seen him in front of the crowd, but could I assume that he would be the same with me personally? Should I respect his position and ignore him? It was the essence of awkwardness.[1]

So many of our children can feel the same way about God: we have made them feel comfortable in the crowd but haven't equipped them to embark on an individual journey with him. Their minds are filled with questions about how and who and what, and if it is even worthwhile. God has given them us to show them an up-close view of what life with God looks like on a day-to-day basis, so that they can see and hear and learn how our relationship with God is done and how it affects us every day.

We do this naturally with other important and personal relationships. We don't fling open the doors and give them all-access passes to view the intimate details of our marriages or our friendships, but we do try to show them the tip of the iceberg of what these healthy relationships should be like. In a marriage, children may get glimpses of their parents being physically affectionate with each other in appropriate ways. They hear how their parents talk to each other and, often, how they talk about each other when one partner isn't around. They are often invited into a little bit of that relationship when they participate in important family discussions or share a group hug. Children and teenagers know that they are only seeing a small part of our relationships and that much more happens out of their sight. If what they hear, see and experience is healthy and life-giving, it gives them not only comfort and security (despite the protests and vomiting noises they may make) but also a knowledge of how to manage close relationships well when they are older.

When a mother is stressed, she may go out for coffee with some of her best friends, to cry and talk. If she comes back happier and more optimistic, her children see the emotional benefit of having good friends to offer love and support. She may share her friends' advice with her partner, and her children hear the difference her friends' influence makes to her. On occasion, the children may be taken along on a group outing to a café or beach, where they see and join in the interactions themselves. Through this experience of watching, listening and participating, they learn what to look for in a friend and how to be a friend to others. Again, they are aware that our friendships go deeper than they can see, but they learn to watch and listen for the benefits of those friendships to us and the way we choose to commit our lives to them.

The problem is that we rarely allow our children similar access to our relationship with God. It can be completely foreign to them. They often know what we believe, and they know that our beliefs steer our lives, but they don't often get to see how our relationship with God works, and in what ways it affects who we are and how we live our lives. If we want our children to connect heart-to-heart with God and gain their identity and purpose from him in a living and active relationship, we need to show them the many tips of the icebergs that exist in our relationship with him. We need to learn how to do bits of our private relationship in a public sphere.

I believe there are four main ways that we can go about modelling our private relationship with God:

- Create windows
- Verbalise more
- Invite
- Overcome the fear

Create windows

To our children, our relationship with God may be shrouded in mystery. Perhaps we disappear into a room to 'spend some time with God', 'have our quiet time' or 'read our Bible notes'. The child may hear some music being played or hear total silence. Sometimes we come out different, sometimes not. For all the child knows, we are dancing naked in there while doing body art, or sleeping, or sitting quietly and staring mindlessly at the wall. On the other hand, God himself may have appeared in bodily form and be having tea and biscuits with us. Our children don't know!

They may be aware that we read the Bible, and may see it occasionally, but they know that we also read joke books and the latest good crime novel. So we like reading—so what? They have no desire to read our *Economist* magazine—it looks boring, and so does the Bible from far away.

Children may hear us say that we want to 'pray about' something, and later they may see that we have made a decision about it, but what exactly happened and when? In their minds, often, praying consists of talking at God. So, really, did we just process the issue out loud with God listening until we made up our mind? Or was it something more? If so, what? And how long did it take?

Do your children even see those little tips of the icebergs—or is your iceberg completely submerged? How would they describe your relationship with God?

The key to creating windows is to allow little glimpses into the various aspects of our personal relationship with God, so that our children and teenagers can see what it looks like to be involved in a two-way relationship with an invisible person. Leave the door ajar when you are having time with God, so they can see that you aren't floating four inches off the ground surrounded in white light. (If you are doing that, it will certainly function as a conversation starter later on!) Seeing a person engage with God is fascinating—even more so if that person is your parent.

If you read your Bible, try doing it in a place where your children can see you. This gives you many opportunities to communicate to them about how you meet God through scripture. My dad used to do this really well. He was a police officer, so he would often come home from a late shift at 2am. Since my bedroom was near the dining room, I would wake to see a bit of light glinting around my door. I would often sit up and look through into the dining room to see him sitting in his normal place, reading the Bible.

Children are naturally nosy, and my dad allowed my nosiness to become an opportunity. He would leave his Bible out on the table, open at the place where he was reading, with his notes next to it. In the morning, I could casually walk past and see what verses he liked, as they were underlined, or I would read his open notebook with his reflections on what the scripture meant to him and how it made him feel. Before that, I had found the Bible desperately boring. I learned how to connect with God through the Bible primarily by sneakily looking through a window into my dad's engagement with God's word. Then I found it so appealing that I wanted to try it.

Remember, these windows exist not to show our children a perfect expression of Jesus but to allow them access to the way our lives entwine with our Father's, and to show them what it looks like when that happens. Jesus was a master at doing this. He taught his disciples not to publicise their giving to the temple, their prayers or their fasting. He taught them to keep these activities between them and God, not between them and the world's approval.[2] But this didn't mean that he hid everything from them. He built windows into his private life with his Father, so that his disciples had a front-row view whenever he chose to give them a glimpse. They knew his habits of fasting and prayer,[3] they knew his patterns of giving,[4] and they overheard his prayers well enough to write them down later.[5] Jesus wasn't allowing them that access so that the disciples would huddle around saying, 'Wow! Jesus is *amazing*. He is the best pray-er I've ever heard. And isn't he holy? I mean, very impressive, really.' He gave them those 'tip of the iceberg' moments so that they could learn a new way of interacting with God their heavenly Father, in relationship, not just as part of the crowd.

Verbalise more

The second main way to model relationship with God requires us to be bolder in sharing verbally about our lives with God. We sometimes assume that children automatically know what is happening, based on what they see, but it is very hard to 'see' a relationship. We need to help them understand our relationship with God by verbally framing experiences for them, debriefing after times of relational significance between us and God, and including them in our current emotional journeys by reflecting out loud in their presence.

Verbally framing

Many people I work with are concerned that if they create a 'window', their children will interrupt their time with God. To children's eyes, we may look as if we are just sitting in a room by ourselves, hanging out. My view, though, is that these 'interruptions' give us the opportunity to frame verbally what is going on. We can now define the reality of the situation, change the way our children perceive what is happening in the room, and explain more about why we value what we are doing. When your child attempts to breach your time, I would suggest you say, 'I'm sorry, darling, God and I are spending some time together. I have some things I want to chat to him about, and I really want to hear what he has to say about them. I love spending time with God, and this is the time he and I set aside to be together just one on one. I'd love to chat to you when we have finished.' You have just shown your child that (a) you are not alone in the room, (b) you and God are interacting right now, and that time is important to you, and (c) you really like hanging out with God. I think that's worth an interruption now and then!

My mother gets a certain look when she is connecting with God in normal everyday life. It's a kind of flicker in her face, but I can't really describe it. I became aware of it only when I was a pre-teenager. When I asked her about it, she told me all about how the Holy Spirit is our guide. She outlined how important to her that connection is in her decisions and how it shapes her feelings about things that are happening to our family. I jokingly began to call her connections with God 'the God-o-meter', but I tuned in really quickly whenever I was talking to her and saw that ever-so-subtle look in her eye. I had never noticed before how often she checked in with God in a day. I was amazed.

As the months and years went by, I began to get jealous. I really, really wanted to hear God's heart and have an internal guide in the way that she had. I wanted access to the wisdom and peace that she had. I tried to use her to get to God. I would tell her about my problems and then ask, 'So what does the God-o-meter say?' I longed for his voice and input. Like a good, empowering mother, though, she would tell me that I had my own 'God-o-meter' and I'd just have to learn to use it. I only began to seek after God's voice in my life because of how she described his impact on hers. She framed those experiences for me so well and so frequently that I noticed them in her life and longed to have them for myself.

This can also be applied to the church setting. As adults, we settle into the way we do things with God, and become familiar with the meaning of certain behaviours, which are expressions of our relationship with God. Silence in church means time to 'reflect' or 'listen to God' or 'silently pray'. To a child, though, it could mean 'big pause' or 'someone forgot what to do'. We need to help them know what is happening, to place a context around the situation—not just so that they can understand our experience, but so that they can engage with it themselves.

In this example, our instinct is perhaps to explain, 'This is the time when we pray and think about Jesus' sacrifice for us.' While that is true, this description only tells the child what the crowd as a whole is 'supposed' to be doing at that moment. It would be much more helpful if we could describe our personal experience in that time: 'This is the time when I remember that I do lots of things wrong, and my heart is so happy that Jesus rescued me. I let my heart and my head tell Jesus all about how much I love him and how he makes me feel.' Then we can invite our children to do the same, encouraging their relationship with him instead of their conformity to a behaviour that they see but don't understand.

This verbal framing helps train children's eyes to see relationship instead of just religious activity. Soon they will notice when you connect with God, because you've put a frame around that connection. You have taught them: when you see this, this is what is happening inside me; this is what God is doing. They will begin to recognise the influence of the presence of God in your life because you have given them a frame in which to see it. Most importantly, they will also know how to enter in.

Debriefing

Most of the time, children are completely unaware of how big a role our relationship with God plays in our daily lives. So much of our relationship is hidden and quiet, as God breaks through into our thoughts and meets us in unexpected places. Our children usually have no idea how we overcome struggles, reach decisions and handle hurts. In part, this is because we rightly wish to protect our children. We are the parents, and we are not to burden them with our problems. But if we never model how to conquer those problems, then we will only be able to give advice, with no fruit to show.

Debriefing is a helpful middle ground in this kind of situation because it means verbalising our experience in retrospect. We don't have to walk our children through the full details of horrible circumstances, nor do we need a deep conversation, but we can share about how our relationship with God carried us through. This can be as simple as leaving the room where we spend our 'quiet times' and plopping down at the meal table, exclaiming, 'Phew, I needed that. I was getting stressed for silly reasons, and I'm sorry for being short with you. Worshipping always gives me such peace, and God reminded me of some things that really helped. Would you please pass the milk?'

Other times are ripe to share a personal story with your child—for example, when they are struggling with a particular situation. One dad told me how he was able to help his teenage son through a very difficult break-up. He said to his son, 'I remember when my first girlfriend broke up with me. I really thought she was the one. I just sat on my bed and cried—no, seriously, really cried hard. Best time I ever had with God, just me crying on a bed and knowing he was in the room with me. He didn't really talk to me or show me anything, but it was so nice to feel him in the room while my heart was all torn up, and know he was there for me. I don't think I talked to anyone for a week. But I got through it, very slowly. I believe in you, son.'

Children also benefit from looking in to a complete story about your journey of decision-making. You can debrief short situations from work. If you had a tough moral decision to make, you can share about it over dinner, telling how God reminded you of a Bible verse that helped you make up your mind, or how scared or embarrassed you were and the way God helped to overcome that feeling. Children need to hear how you think and make decisions with God alongside you.

Invite

The third main way to model our relationship with God is to invite children into our experience, to view it close up and possibly participate in it. This doesn't mean bringing them into a corporate experience, but inviting them to engage with God personally in parallel with us. That way, our children can watch us do it, and have a go themselves in a safe environment.

If you have a time of connecting with God at home, your 'quiet time', why not invite your children in with you, once in a while?

You can lay the boundaries firmly, for example: 'This is my time with God and I love connecting my heart to his. If you would like to join me, you can spend time with God on your own too. There are some colouring pens here if you want to draw pictures that God gives you, or if you want to write him a letter. I'm going to be over there, singing and reading my Bible and chatting to God and listening to him. If you get bored, or when you have finished, feel free to leave!'

One of the women in my 'Parenting for Faith' course decided to do this with her daughter. Her favourite time with God was when she was walking her dog. It was her chance to enjoy his presence, share her heart, intercede for her family and have God minister to her. Her teenage daughter grew up knowing that this was her mum's time with God, and understood how valuable it was to her. One day, the mum invited her daughter to come and spend time with God alongside her. For the next year, they engaged with God together, walking side by side in silence, both individually connecting to God but feeling that they were sharing his presence with one another. It was something they both cherished, and it often opened up conversations later in the day about what God was doing in their lives.

You can apply this idea in many ways. Offer your children the option to stay in the main service with you instead of going out to the children's group at church. Frame why you worship and what God does in you when you worship. Invite them to try it for themselves, next to you, as you worship with the congregation. At home, you could grab your son or daughter while you are reading your Bible, and ask what they think a certain verse means for your relationship with a colleague who is really annoying you.

Overcome the fear

The most common struggle, for the people I work with, is a concern that their own relationship with God isn't good enough. They want their children to have a wonderful relationship with God—better than they themselves may have—and some of them feel inadequate to model it because of a sense of failure.

I understand that fear! I have that fear all the time. What we have to remember is that we are not trying to model perfection; we are trying to model the reality of a life in relationship with God, pursuing him and growing in him. I want my child to have a closer relationship with God than I have, but I don't have to have it all worked out. I just have to be one step ahead of him, so that I can show him where to put his feet. It's the same with all parenting. If we want our children not to yell when they are angry, we need to climb on top of our own issues with anger. Does that mean we have to have the problem completely sorted before we address it with our children? No, we just have to be moving forward in our journey and be talking to our children, modelling what to do when they fail: how to put things right; how to keep trying and get better.

If you want to model encountering God through the Bible, but you are fearful that you don't manage this well yourself, I would suggest that you commit yourself to exploring how you best connect with the Bible, until you find that you are consistently meeting with God when you read it. When that happens, start creating the window for your children. Begin to verbalise how helpful you find it to read the Bible, how you hear God speak to you through it, and how excited you are that you are doing it. Remember, you're not modelling the discipline of reading every day; you are modelling relationship with God through encountering his word. If you miss a day, don't feel the need to admonish yourself verbally about your failure, as that will communicate to your children that you are trying to achieve a goal in a task. It would be better if you voiced how sad you are that you missed your time connecting with God, and how it has affected you emotionally and spiritually throughout the day.

We too are on a journey, and we need to pursue what we want our children to pursue. This may require big changes in us. We can't just want better for our children; we need to blaze the trail.

Questions for reflection

• What has been your experience of learning how to have an individual relationship with God? Who have you learned from?
• What aspects of your relationship with God can you create a window into?
• How do you think your children will respond to being invited into aspects of your relationship with God? What do you need to think through, to ensure that you are comfortable and confident enough to offer the invitation?

Notes

1. I ended up blurting out 'We went swimming' for some reason, just in case I came across as having wandered down from a recent shower to hang out in the lobby. He smiled and we engaged in small talk until the senior staff mercifully arrived. I kick myself to this day for not taking advantage of the opportunity to have a real conversation with him.
2. Matthew 6:1–18
3. Matthew 14:23
4. Matthew 17:24
5. John 17

*

— Chapter 3 —

Tying together truth and experience

I followed her out of the Sunday group room as she slammed the door behind her. Her three-year-old brother had just died, and her world had been turned upside down. Eleven-year-old Gwynneth scowled at me, 'I know all of this stuff!' She said, waving her arms, 'It's not like any of it matters anyway. I memorised these stupid verses and I've heard the story of Noah a billion times. And don't tell me God loves me, blah blah blah. It doesn't mean anything!' Tears poured down Gwynneth's face and her whole body shook with anger. She so needed to connect with God's comfort and love, but none of her knowledge was helping her find him.

Moments of need often expose the cracks in our faith. Gwynneth realised how disconnected she actually was from God when she discovered how little her knowledge helped her at the point where she needed him most. What she needed was relationship, and she didn't have it. But a relationship with God isn't just for crisis points; it is for every moment of every day. There is so much on offer for us when we live in relationship with God: his joy, his guidance, his companionship, his strength and power, his love and truth. Living in connection with God provides a relationship that helps us grow and sustains us through all the good and bad times of our lives.

In order to help our children to grow into a connected relationship with God, we need to look at how good relationships develop. Relationship requires many things, two of which are knowledge and experience. People who read my CV may gain some information about me, but they still want to meet me in an interview, to match their knowledge about me with the experience of what I am actually like so that we can begin to build a relationship. Other people might meet me casually at a party or conference. In order to deepen their experience of my personality and build relationship, they converse with me, growing their knowledge of me by sharing personal information and stories. This is how we, as humans, build relationship and maintain it. We grow in our knowledge and experience of people, and thus grow closer and deeper in relationship. Eventually, we might add in a personal commitment to deliberately extend that process, and *voilá*! We are developing and maintaining deep, connected friendships and relationships.

Unfortunately, many times we don't follow that process in growing our children's relationship with God. Children love learning and absorb information so quickly that it is easy to feed their quest for knowledge with information about God. We encourage them to know about God, and that is a great thing to do. Eventually, we may encourage them to meet him in worship or prayer, with varying levels of success. Very often, though, knowledge of God and experience of him are kept separate. The key to relationships, as we have seen, is connecting the two. Knowledge of a person informs the way we experience them, and our experience of them informs our knowledge. One without the other is incomplete.

God meant our relationship with him to work in the same way—for knowledge about him and experience of him to go hand in hand. When asked by a teacher of the law which commandment was the most important, Jesus replied, 'The most important one says: "People of Israel, you have only one Lord and God. You must love him with all your heart, soul, mind, and strength."'[1] This is a holistic way of loving, involving everything in us—our emotions, our choices, our will, our understanding and our determination. But often we grow in only one or two of these aspects of love, and keep them disconnected from each other.

God's plan for how we should relate to him ties in with the way we normally process and absorb truth. It is natural for us to weigh truth against experience, and experience against truth. If you told me that blue Smarties float, I would not just accept that claim as a fact. I'd want to test it out. Conversely, if I myself noticed that blue Smarties spontaneously drifted toward the sky when out of their package, I would want to know why. 'Does this happen with everything blue? Or just blue Smarties? Am I going crazy?' I would want to find out the truth behind my experience.

We do the same in relationships. We tell our children that we love them, but they test out that truth in their experiences with us. They want to know if we still love them when they are naughty or disappointing, or when they fail. They test out the truth of our love and eventually grow to feel secure in it. Their experience in relationship matches the truth of our love, and the truth of our love is made evident in their experience.

Too often, we don't allow our children to go through the same process with God. We feed them information about God but don't guide them to experience the truth of it in relationship. Conversely, if they have an experience with God, we might forget to guide them to the biblical truth behind that encounter, which would anchor the experience for them. This happens to us as adults, too, and the result is that our natural human desires try to make connections between truth and relational experience for us, often in unhelpful or misrepresentative ways.

Truth without experience

If we know biblical truth but haven't been guided to see how that truth will work out in our experience of relationship with God, we often make wrong assumptions about what it should look like in experience. This is a prime reason why children struggle with their faith in the pre-teen years. The biblical truth that they have been taught doesn't seem to be true at all when compared with their experience. But this is often because they are functioning out of wrong assumptions instead of the reality of what that truth means in dynamic, two-way relationship with God. For example:

- Biblical truth: God has a plan.[2]
- Relational assumption: Everything that happens to me is part of his plan, and I shouldn't do anything until I am sure that it is part of God's plan.

- Biblical truth: God is loving.[3]
- Relational assumption: Nothing bad should happen to me or anyone I love because he loves me.

- Biblical truth: God knows everything.[4]
- Relational assumption: I don't have to tell him how I feel, or share with him in prayer, because he knows it already.

If we look at just these three biblical truths about God, we can see a vast difference between the assumptions that follow them and God's designed reality.

The God-designed reality is that God has wonderful plans for us that we can choose to take part in. But he also gave us free will, as well as desires and dreams of what we want to accomplish in our lives that he wants to bless.[5]

God loves us, but his love doesn't mean that he puts us in a bubble to isolate us from the world. It means that he is committed to living in relationship with us, comforting, guiding, strengthening and encouraging us as we walk together through life. Things will go wrong in our lives that he didn't cause, and we will make poor choices that affect us badly, but, because he loves us, he promises that he will work them together for our good.[6]

Although God knows everything—our thoughts, our hearts, our actions—from the beginning of time he has forged a way for us to have a relationship with him, even sacrificing his Son, because he longs for us to want to be with him and share our lives with him. He has sacrificed so much just for a two-way relationship with us.

No wonder many of our children struggle with their faith, when the knowledge of God we give them leads to wrong expectations about their experience of him, which actually disconnect them from him and result in disappointment. The truth that they know should be drawing them closer into relationship with him as they see it reflected in their experience.

Experience without truth

On the other hand, if we simply validate children's experiences and perceptions of God without grounding them in biblical truth, then we are enabling them to invent 'truth' out of their experience. When I was a child, my mum always made me eat the crusts on my sandwiches. Based on my experiences—that this was important to my mother, and that crusts had a particularly unappealing taste—I formed some assumed 'truths' about crusts. In summary, I believed that the crust of bread held more nutrients in it than the rest of the bread. The more types of bread I saw and tasted, the more I felt confirmed in my belief. I passed this 'truth' on to children I worked with and insisted it to be truth when talking to my friends. I would force myself to eat crusts to ensure that I was benefitting from all the nutrients held in them. Embarrassingly, I made it to the age of 26 before I discovered that my assumed truths about bread crusts were not, in fact, true!

Although this may seem a silly example, we can do the same thing if we encourage too much experience of God without the underlying biblical truth. In this kind of situation, children will draw their own conclusions about the underlying truth and then apply it to other aspects of their relationship with God. For example:

- **Experience:** Some people hear God speak occasionally.
- **Truth assumption:** He doesn't speak very often. His speech is very unpredictable. And if he does speak to others and not very much to me, then he must be cross with me or doesn't care about me.

- Experience: My world is falling apart.
- Truth assumption: God has abandoned me or is punishing me.

- Experience: I had a wonderful time with God at the church retreat/conference/camp.
- Truth assumption: It was a 'mountain top' experience that doesn't happen in the real everyday world.

These kinds of experience are very poignant and very real to children, but, if no one helps them to connect their experiences to biblical truths, they may create assumed truths that aren't found in the Bible. Assumed truths lead to a wrong view of God and result in a disconnected relationship with him. Real biblical truths, by contrast, lead to a rooting in him that guides, informs and increases a healthy relationship with God.

The underlying biblical truth is that God is constantly speaking, and he promises that we will grow to recognise and know his voice.[7] He promises to be with us and walk with us through our struggles, comforting and encouraging us.[8] His presence and closeness are for the everyday, and we can enjoy him wherever we are, in whatever circumstance.[9] Many children struggle because we don't help them to measure and deepen their experiences with God by rooting them in biblical truth.

In order to grow a healthy relationship, we need a good balance of truth and relational experience. It is important that we learn to wrap one around the other, viewing one in the context of the other, so that they are inextricably linked, instead of compartmentalising them as separate elements. When we help our children to learn biblical truth about God, we can wrap around it the relational effects of that truth and help them experience it in their relationship with him. When our children have an encounter with God or are wondering about their life circumstances, we can help them understand their experience by placing biblical truth at the centre, to anchor their minds as well as their hearts. This will enable their relationship with God to be fruitful and growing, with every aspect reflecting the truth and reality of life with him.

Proactively tying together truth and experience

Modelling

Modelling is very important, however you choose to expand your children's knowledge to affect their experience. Find times in your schedule to verbalise more of how your knowledge of God impacts your experience of him. Create windows in which your children can see you having an experience with God or processing a life circumstance, referring to the Bible to ground you. Be open about the Bible passages that influence your thoughts and life choices.

Bible stories

So often, Bible stories are wonderful and exciting for our children at first, but quickly become stale. When we tell these stories, we often focus heavily on the actions of the people involved and only peripherally on God's. To a great extent, this is in the nature of the biblical narrative. For example, in the story of David and Goliath, God's part is implied but not described directly. In the story of Joshua and the battle of Jericho, God's angel appears to Joshua beforehand but we just assume that God is the one who knocks down the walls. We can often forget that God is a character in the story.

If your child seems to know every Bible story, try inviting him or her to tell it to you from God's point of view. What was God doing, thinking and feeling during the story? Most Bible stories give us some clues, and the rest we can work out from our knowledge of God's character. This is a great way of helping children to see the relationship between God and the people in the Bible, and then applying this knowledge so that they learn how a relationship with

God works in everyday life. It will also give you a further insight into how your child views God. You may need to show them how to do it the first couple of times, but after a while your children will really begin to fly.

Another good idea is to add new stories to your child's knowledge base. We may feel that we are stuck with the stories in children's picture Bibles, but there are many other wonderful stories in the Bible that can add depth to our relationships with God. You can be strategic in your approach, adding stories into the repertoire that you feel may be helpful to your child's current situation. As you tell a story, include God in the narrative and weave in an understanding of how the characters' relationships with God affected their choices.

After I've told a story like this, I encourage children to make me a story book with pictures in it. We pick out seven or eight key scenes and each child illustrates a few. This is a great way of reinforcing the story and gives you a book that you can read again and again, including their own pictures. You can also encourage your children to draw God into the illustrations, to remind them of where God was and what he was doing during the story.

Don't feel trapped into telling just Old Testament stories. There are some wonderful stories in Acts, and you can even turn some of Paul's letters into a story. For example, Galatians is a rollicking ride! The letter kicks off with Paul feeling really angry because other people have been coming into the church and confusing the believers, so Paul launches into a story of how he came to tell the message about Jesus. You could tell the story and invite your child to participate in it. The Galatians were confused about a lot of things, so Paul sets them straight. What would your child say to the Galatians to help them over their confusion about having to earn their way into heaven? How would he or she explain it to them? You could role-play the conversation together, you playing the part of a foolish Galatian and your child acting as Paul. (Don't forget to ask 'Paul' how he came to believe in Jesus.) You could use the story to help children to practise sharing about the difference a relationship with God makes to them, and why it is important for other people. Feel free to make it difficult! I once had the privilege of doing this with a family at their home, and the oldest brother (the 'Galatian') refused to convert, no matter what his nine-year-old sister ('Paul') said. She passionately testified about her life with God, pleaded with him, took every question and answered it, and even attempted to pray for him. I've never seen a family so engaged in a debate about how the truth we believe affects our relationship with God.

Memorising Bible verses

Many of our children memorise Bible verses at church and at home, through actions and songs. Memorising Bible verses is wonderful. How often are we helped by being reminded of God's word in our daily lives? It is a powerful relational tool, but it can become stale and unconnected to any experience of God in our child's life. There are several ways we can grow that connection between knowledge and experience. For example, if there are some key verses that are very important to you and your relationship with God, try displaying them somewhere in your home. You can take the opportunity to describe to your children why these verses are important to you and your relationship with God, and why you like to remind yourself of them.

If you actively work on memorising Bible verses with your children, try returning to the ones they know and discussing their relational significance. Often, verses that we memorise as commands are actually promises that can dramatically impact our relationship with God. Take, for example, Psalm 119:105: 'Your word is a lamp that gives light wherever I walk.' Many children perceive this as a command and come away with the view that it is important to read the Bible because 'God said so'. But actually this verse is a promise that God's word will bring help, direction and light to the times and places in our lives where we feel lost and scared. What a relief!

When memorising Bible verses, I would suggest that you choose verses of encouragement and promises that help to feed a child's relationship with God, so that the Bible is increasingly showing what a life with God is like. Make sure to tie your child's learning into experience by reading Bible stories and telling stories from your own life that reflect the biblical promises. So often, we think the tie is obvious when it isn't!

Laying a framework for life experiences

Sometimes it is life experiences that most badly shake our belief in the reality of relationship with God. When the big difficulties arise in life, it is vastly helpful to know that our children have those truth and experience 'ties' in place, so that their life circumstances fit into the framework they already have—we don't need to try desperately to build a framework around their circumstances. As adults, we can see most big issues coming, even if only a little bit ahead of time. It may be a family crisis: a divorce, bankruptcy, a big move, a death in the family or a loved one's illness. It may be a difficult life experience for our child, such as a new school, bullying, difficulty with reading or friendship issues.

When we guess that a particular issue might arise, we can begin to prepare our children for it without necessarily explaining it fully. When I was four, my mother began to build a framework for me of how friendship might work in my first year of full-time school. I remember her chatting to me about how girls in school might say, 'If you don't do this, I won't be your friend any more' or 'If you were a real friend, you would do this.' She told me that real friends are much better than fake friends, and that girls who say such things will only be fake friends. She explored with me what real friends are like, and what I should say to girls who were trying to be mean to me to force me to do something. At the time, my experiences didn't reflect those types of friendships at all, but my mum wanted to build a framework for me before my experience needed it. A year later, when girls at school began to do what she'd described, I instantly identified where that experience fitted into my framework, responded in the way I knew to respond, and got on with my life with fantastic, solid friends. I watched other children, though, being manipulated by those girls because they had no foundation to know how to understand the situation and respond positively.

We can prepare a solid, tied-together truth-and-experience spiritual framework for our children's life circumstances. Then, when difficulties arise, they can identify the situation and how to cope with it, without letting it rock their understanding or relationship with God. For example, if we know that a big move is coming up for our family, we can begin to think through the spiritual framework that our children will need to help them grow closer in relationship with God, and begin to build it in advance. For the few months before, we could casually read stories from the Bible about people who have made big moves—like Abraham, Moses and even Jesus—and discuss what they felt like and what God was doing in their lives while the move was happening. We could begin to look at biblical promises about God being with us, giving us the desires of our heart, and giving us hope.

Expanding relational experiences with God

It is important that children not only know about God but are meeting with him, sharing their hearts and hearing his voice. If your children haven't experienced that, they are missing out on the key part of relationship—relating! It is so crucial that all children do not just know about God but know how to access him in prayer, worship and relationship. We will be discussing the practicalities of how to encourage this experience in our children in the next section of the book.

This kind of engagement is particularly helpful in connecting truth to relationship because it makes the truth real. Our children may know that God says he will comfort or help them, but that knowledge becomes real only when they are comforted by him and recognisably helped by him in relationship. The truth of our knowledge is proven in relationship, and we must give our children the opportunity to experience that.

Questions for reflection

- In your life, have truth and experience of God always been tied together? How has this impacted your relationship with God?
- In what areas do you think you have done well in tying together truth and experience of God for your children? What areas could be expanded?
- Is anything coming up in your children's lives that you need to help prepare them for?

Notes
1.   Mark 12:29–30
2.   Jeremiah 29:11
3.   Psalm 42:8; 57:3; John 3:16
4.   Psalm 147:4–5; Acts 15:16–18
5.   Psalm 37:4
6.   Romans 8:28
7.   Jeremiah 33:3; Job 33:13–14; John 10:2–5, 14–15
8.   Psalm 23
9.   John 14:16; Matthew 28:20

*

Part Two

Connecting children to God's heart

We all know that our children's lives are not easy. They ride extreme emotional rollercoasters every day and have to process massive amounts of learning, physically, mentally, spiritually and socially. Children's lives are complicated by family situations, stress at school, and everyday pressures. Their relationships anchor them in this whirlwind and give them identity and purpose.

Essentially, a relationship with God can help our children to cope with daily life and shape them into the people they have been designed to be. God is the ultimate anchor in their lives and only he has the power to bring them the peace, strength, healing, identity and purpose they need to flourish. In order to build this relationship, we need to help them grow to be God-connected, not just God-smart. Knowledge about God will not comfort them when they cry or help them when they are lonely. Only a God-connected life can do that.

My husband is a great person. I could tell you all about him: I have endless stories of his silliness, his kindness, his selflessness, the childishness of his jokes, the joy he brings me every day, his smile and laugh, his constant support and love. I could overwhelm you with stories and you could 'know' him through them. You might even feel vaguely fond of him, even though you had never met him, just because of the picture you managed to conjure in your head, based on my description. But I do not believe that you would have understood the tiniest fraction of who he really is or what it is like to be in a relationship with him: what his face looks like when he is sad or what it feels like to have him pray for you, be cheered by him, or to have him lovingly put your socks on because you are too unwell to do it yourself. Being in a relationship with him is totally different from knowing information about him. Being in relationship with someone is something that we can attempt to describe, but the description will never compare to the fullness of the experience.

We are called to train and grow God-connected children, so that they can reap all the benefits of being in relationship with him. This section will help us free our children from things that may be holding them back from connecting with God, and give us the tools to guide them into a pattern of life that consists of a two-way relationship with God. We will look at how we can pray with our children in ways that empower and build up their relationship with God. Children need and deserve what God designed for all of us: a life full of his voice, his healing, his words, his love, his direction, his joy, his grace and provision, his presence and his power. We can help them enter into it.

*

Chapter 4

Unwinding wrong views of God

I looked out over 200 bored faces. I was teaching 'prayer' to eight-
and nine-year-old children at a summer conference, and it did not
look as if it would go well. They were bored as soon as they knew
the topic—but I knew that wouldn't last long. I began to ask them
to explore with me what prayer is and how we do it. With rolled
eyes, answers began to come in. We gathered a very extensive list.
According to the children, the general guidelines of prayer are as
follows:

* Prayer is talking to God about specific things you want to bring
  to his attention.
* Primarily included in each prayer should be a 'sorry' section, a
  'thank you' section, and a 'please' section, unless it is a grace
  prayer for meal-times, or an absolute emergency—when 'please
  help' becomes enough and you are off the hook for the 'sorry'
  and 'thank you'.
* In general, you need to sit still and be quiet, close your eyes, fold
  your hands, start with 'Dear God' and end with 'Amen'.
* God is always available to hear you, and you can do this type
  of prayer any time, but you have to wait for a while to see the
  results, if there are any.

I asked if they had any questions about prayer, and not a hand was
raised. Nope, it seemed they had it all sorted.

With a smile, I asked them what they would think if I told them
that they didn't have to do any of the things they'd listed. What if
I told them that they could tell jokes to God, cry in front of him,

watch TV with him, ask him questions and hear his answers? What would happen if they didn't sit still or close their eyes or say 'Dear God' and 'Amen' when they prayed?

There was a huge pause and the little heads started shaking a universal 'no'. They smiled uncomfortably and visually checked with the other leaders to see if anyone was going to stone me for my obvious heresy. One boy piped up, 'If you don't do those things that we put on the board, then it's not prayer! It won't work!' The group erupted in agreement: hand after hand shot up in the air. After several minutes of listening to the general discussion on why it wouldn't work, one brave girl raised her hand. 'I'm not sure if it would be OK to do what you say, but if it was… I'd really, really like it and would maybe like to do it more. Praying would be totally different, like having a friend instead of talking to God.'

I have done this seminar with thousands of children across England and Europe, and their answers continually come back the same. Somehow, we have given a very specific view of prayer to our children, and they have become stuck in a way of interacting with God that actually separates them from him. They have received this view from us—their parents or prime carers, children's leaders and churches. We have spun them an image of prayer and how to engage with it, and we need proactively to unwind it again so that our children can be free. Otherwise, we are just trying to build on crumbly soil with little foundation. We need to make sure we help them build firm foundations on which they can base their relationship with God.

In many children there exists a disconnection between what is told to them about prayer and their experience of it. We tell children, 'God is always listening', 'You can pray to him at any time about anything' and 'God loves you'. They know all these statements and will repeat them back with an insistence that they believe them. The problem is that they don't see these biblical truths worked out in their experience of God through prayer or in their life circumstance. Most children don't feel connected, loved and accepted in prayer. That is partly because of their own personal experience of God and their life circumstances, and partly because we have helped shape their experience of prayer into a rigid, often one-way message delivery system from them to God.

As we discussed in the previous chapter, often our children's experiences lead them to assume certain false 'truths' about who God is and how relationship works with him. These assumptions create a picture of God that pushes many children away from wanting to be in relationship with him, causing disconnection. In order to want to be in relationship and share our life with someone, we have to like that person. We have to know who they are and how our relationship will work, and then decide if we want to go ahead with it. A big part of the reason why children don't want to connect with God is that they have created a wrong (and unappealing) view of who he is and what a relationship with him would be like.

Sometimes it is hard to get children to articulate this feeling because the 'right' answers, the assumed biblically true answers, are so ingrained in their heads that most children aren't aware that there is a discrepancy. Once I organised a group of children to explore this idea by making two lists. On one flipchart page we collected ideas about what God is like, and on the other one we collected ideas about what God felt like to us, both in his character and in our relationship with him. The lists were vastly different, and the children were so surprised. Let's look at it from an adult's point of view. It's no good you telling me that the boss whom you and I share is gracious, loving, encouraging and fantastic if my experience of him has been that he is rude, unreachable, critical and unreasonably disapproving. To me, that is who he is, and I will shape all of my interactions with him accordingly.

The positive side to this issue is that once we can identify the false assumed truths and false relational assumptions that have shaped a wrong view of God and relationship with him, we can begin to unwind it proactively. We can help to correct this view of relationship and prayer, tying together the solid heart-to-heart connection with God and the knowledge of biblical truths that we hope to release in our children.

I would like to explore four of the most common views that children hold. Although this is by no means a complete list, it will enable us to help with any view of God that our children may create. Children often switch between views, or even hold two or three different views in parallel in their minds. Most children won't fit completely into one category or another, but it is helpful to explore the different views so that we can see how to correct our children's course towards a healthier and more accurate view of God, enabling them to relate to him fully. As we look at each of these general views, I will highlight the ways in which we unconsciously contribute to or reinforce them, and also how to unwind them if they are present.

'Distant God' view

Sometimes he is happy, sometimes he isn't; either way, this God tends to be uninterested in us, as he is busy doing very important things. Children who hold this view can feel unimportant and believe that they are bothering God when they talk to him. They feel they should 'save' their requests until there is a really big one, because God doesn't have the time to spare to deal with all our little issues. Praying is very stressful for them as they feel that if they take too long, or say things wrong, God will get impatient, so they often opt for an adult to do the praying.

Unwinding the 'distant God' view

The 'distant God' is a very common view among children, as many of our books and songs unwittingly contribute to an image of God that places him physically distant from us. Art and movies show God in the clouds above us, wrapped up in his world of heaven, busy doing things. We often look up or point up when referring to God, and many songs refer to God 'looking down on us' from above. It is not hard, therefore, to see where the 'distant God' view comes from.

We may have reinforced this view simply by praying at a normal pace, when our child prays much more slowly. We may jump in during 'prayer time' to help our children complete the thought or finish sooner. They pay attention to how we pray: to children, it can sound as if we are talking faster than they are, which implies that prayer time needs to hurry up a bit or that God doesn't want to be kept waiting. Often, a child will confuse our impatience with God's impatience.

We may also have fed into this view by dismissing something that our child wants to pray about: football, healing for their little teeny scratch on the knee, or their desire for a trip to Disneyland. We may casually say, 'Oh no, let's think of something else to pray about' or 'I doubt God cares about the results of the football match.' As silly as it seems, these comments build into a very distant view of God.

We can begin to unwind the 'distant God' view by proactively bringing to our child's attention God's promise that he is with us always, and exploring with them what that promise means about God and our relationship with him. We can talk about pictures or songs that contribute to the view that God is far away, and ask them why they think people portray God like that. Moving to the next step, we can ask them to redraw the picture, or discuss how the song could be changed to make it more like the truth.

Unwinding this view will also involve modelling how to live in relationship with God with the right view. We may need to be aware of our language, to hear if we are accidentally reinforcing the distant view of God. Even if we are pushed for time in prayer, it is helpful to slow our speech to the pace of our child's and make sure prayer times are very casual. We don't need to be afraid of long pauses. If children are struggling, a simple 'Take your time, God really wants to hear what you want to say, and he loves waiting to hear all of it!' may help to relax them. Instead of dismissing 'silly' prayer points, why not encourage them to share with God: 'You know, I'm sure

God would love to hear what you think about that. Why don't you tell him?'

'Happy optimistic God' view

Super-nice; super-jolly; super-passive: this version of God smiles through whatever happens. He sits back and enjoys the worship we send him and has a clichéd response to everything. On the surface, this view of God doesn't seem too harmful, but children's reactions to it create two distinct responses.

On the one hand, there are children who forge a pleasing 'performance' attitude towards God and major heavily on asking for things in prayer. They attempt to charm God by their goodness, so that he will favour them with good things. They can be very competitive with other children, trying to be the 'best', seeking God's approval as their glittering personalities earn them currency to spend.

On the other hand, some children can be dismissive and disconnected in their response to this God. They can see him as being petty and playing 'favourites'. If they have low self-esteem, they feel as if they could never compete with the good children for his affection and favour. His perceived jolliness means that they often feel he doesn't care about the realities of their lives and the difficulties they experience. He holds no answers for their deep questions, and he doesn't tolerate sadness, anger or pain for very long. His goal is to make us jolly, like him, and many children can't connect with that idea.

Unwinding the 'happy optimistic God' view

We can feed into this view of God in many ways. Often, especially with younger children, we focus on the nice things about him (God is loving, God is caring, God is happy) and on what God wants us to do (God wants us to obey, be kind, share). Developmentally, children at this age are learning about cause and effect, and sometimes these two ideas become paired together: God loves us because we obey, are kind and share; therefore, if we don't do those things, then God will stop loving, caring and being happy with us.

We can begin to unwind the 'happy optimistic' view by adding some helpful relational truth to our times together, using Bible stories that show other aspects of God. Read the parable of the prodigal son together and explain that, just like the father in the story, God loves us no matter what we do. Even if we have done something wrong, God really wants to run to us and hug us and help us change, so that we can live close together again. We can also ensure that we focus less on what God wants us to do and more on how to do relationship with him. Try using 'when' statements: 'When I feel lonely, God is with me'; 'When I feel scared, God protects me.' This builds an understanding of God and of relationship, and still works with the cause-and-effect awareness that the child's brain is processing.

Another thing we sometimes do that endorses the 'happy optimistic' view of God is to answer children's questions or difficulties with glib answers, excuses or clichés: 'I know he's annoying you, but God loves him too, so you need to be nice to him', 'Smile, Jesus loves you', 'You just need to have faith' or 'God will make it all right in the end.' These statements tend to invalidate our children's emotional experiences and infer that God wants, first and foremost, for them to get over their pain quickly and return to a happy-go-lucky emotional state. Children need to know that God walks with them in their pain and sees the reality of their situations. They don't need short answers; they need a way to connect with God.

Try validating the child's situation and sharing a bit of what you would do in the situation, ending by referring your child to a connection to God. 'I know he's annoying you, but God loves him too, so you need to be nice to him' can turn into 'It sounds as if you are getting really angry and stressed. When I feel like that, I like to take a short loo break[1] and talk to God about it all. He really helps me calm down and work out what to do. Do you want to take a break?' You can take the opportunity later to debrief on the situation and talk about how God loves us even in difficult circumstances. At that moment, though, the child needs an emotional, relational connection with God, not a command from him of what to do.

We can also contribute to the 'happy optimistic' view if we are not modelling the reality of a full life with God for our children. If we don't let them know how God ministers to us in those confusing, angry or sad places, they may not yet know that aspect of his work. Unwinding this wrong view may be as simple as beginning to model how God partners with you in your life, and encouraging your child to trust him to do the same.

'Angry God' view

He sits in the sky on his throne of judgment, critically watching every moment of our day to spot our sins. When he sees one, his anger flashes and punishment pours out. He is easily offended and requires everyone around him to be as perfect as possible. This view of God produces fear in children and a desperate need to perform. He is impossible to please, so the stress for them is on doing what God says to avoid his displeasure. Love rarely enters into it. Relationship with this God is not desired, as the whole goal is to keep our head down and try to avoid being seen.

Unwinding the 'angry God' view

None of us ever wants to communicate this view of God to our children. Nevertheless, some of the things we do can contribute to a version of it. For example, many of us accidentally overemphasise 'saying sorry to God' when our children do wrong things. On the surface, this is a good thing: confession is biblical and is important for keeping us close to God. Unfortunately, it can contribute to a view of sin that drives children away from God instead of towards him.

We often simplify the concept of sin, explaining it as something we do wrong that hurts God, so we have to apologise and then God can forgive us. If we think about this, though, we are really saying that when we sin, it is like kicking God in the shins. He is hurt, and a bit upset, and we need to say 'sorry' in the same way that we do with our friends, and then everyone gets along again. This can imply that God sits around feeling a bit resentful until we finally manage to apologise, and then he has to forgive us because of what Jesus did. God sighs and rolls his eyes and says 'fine', and then everyone goes back to playing, just a little more warily.

Children can grow to expect that God is always feeling a bit hurt or resentful towards them, unless they can stay on top of apologising enough or not sinning. So how do we unwind this view of God? I believe that the main way is by changing our view of sin and the way we communicate it to children.

The following is a long example, but I hope it helps to present an alternative picture for you to use with your children. I describe sin to children as something that gets in the way between us and God. It's like a small child sitting in a sandbox eating sand. The sand isn't good for her, and it's all over her face and in her mouth. She is choking and coughing, but still loves being in the sandbox. What's even worse is that her father has built a wonderful huge playground for her to play in, and has a big ice cream cone for her to eat. He sees her eating the sand and runs over to her, saying, 'No! That's bad for you! Stop eating sand! Come over here and I'll clean you up and we can play together and you can eat this ice cream. It will be so much fun!'

But the little girl won't come. The father feels sad and says firmly to her, 'Stop eating sand! It's bad for you! Come with me and play!' The girl's face turns angry and she says, 'No!' The father's heart gets more distressed and more frustrated. He hates the sand because it is getting in the way, stopping his daughter from being together with him. He is sad that she keeps choosing the sand over all the great stuff he has for her, but he won't make her come away. She has to choose.

She finally gets tired and fed up with her struggles in the sand. She pauses for a moment and looks up at her heartbroken father, filled with love for her, and sees all the wonderful things he has created for her and him to do together. Her eyes widen as she realises what she has been doing and what she has been missing. She decides she wants to get out of the sandbox. And, of course, as soon as she lifts her dirty arms to her father, he lets out a whoop of joy, swoops her up and washes her with water that cleans all the dirt away. She and her father can now enjoy each other and all the wonderful things he has prepared for her.

God hates sin because, just like the inedible sand, it is bad for us. It distracts and separates us from him, our Father, and all he has for us in relationship with him. So when we sin—when we try to eat sand—is he ready to squash us because he is angry with us? No! His heart is sad because he wants the best for us, and we are choosing things that hurt us and steal away our time with him and our closeness to him. When we realise that we are sinning and say, 'I'm done. I don't want to do this any more', he sweeps us up and cleans us.

Before Jesus came, the sand stuck to us and we couldn't get free, but, because of what Jesus did on the cross, he provided the water that can wash every piece of sin-sand away. So do we need to say sorry to God? Well, we need to say, 'Father God, I want out. I'm sad I did this and I want you to clean me again so that we can be together.' If you want to say sorry to God because he was so concerned for you and his heart was sad because of the way you were hurting yourself, then you can, but he's just so happy and proud of you for choosing to get out of the sand!

This view of sin and how it affects our view of God is helpful for children in taking away the perception of an angry, displeased

God and replacing it with the correct view of a God who is on our side, wants the best for us, and is sad when we choose to do things that hurt us. That's a God with whom children want to be in relationship.[2]

'Unpredictable God' view

He is mysterious and changeable. We never know how he is going to react, and we can't guess his plan. At first, children struggle angrily with this God, but eventually respond with defeat and dismissal. In their view, God will do what he wants when he wants, so there isn't much point in trying to persuade him or even being around him. Most circumstances they see, good or bad, happen because of God, so they don't know fully how to feel about him. They can feel like victims to God's whims, and feel under pressure from adults to accept their fate with contentment. They rarely want to invest in relationship with this God because they know they want people they can count on, and this God isn't one of them.

Unwinding the 'unpredictable God' view

We can feed into this view by overemphasising submission to God's will and to his mysteries. We sometimes tell children, 'God works in mysterious ways', 'God has a bigger plan' or 'One day we will know why God did this.' How do we unwind such a view? I think it's important to help children to remind themselves of what they do know, as a basis for processing the things they don't understand.

One boy I worked with had a mum with cancer, and his father was desperate to know how to help him connect with God about it. The child's grandparents and family friends were giving him all the above 'assurances', which were making him wobble enormously in his view of God.

Instead, I encouraged the father to chat honestly to his son and model for him how he himself was processing the experience. He ended up having a deep conversation with his son, saying, 'I don't know why Mum has cancer. I don't think God gave it to her, because that doesn't fit with the loving Father God that I know in the Bible and in my life. I'm not sure there is a "why". I think we live in a world that got broken by sin and evil, and it's not yet fixed and perfect in the way that it will be in heaven. Your mum has cancer, and we are all scared and upset about it. What do I know? I know that God loves me and you and your mum and has promised in the Bible that he will walk with us through everything in our lives. He has promised that he will take away our fear and will fill us with his love. With every tear we cry, he is right there, catching them and storing them up; he is right here, comforting us and helping us. I know that and I believe that. It helps me to chat to him about how I feel and to listen to what he says back to me about it. I don't feel alone when I'm with God. In the meantime, the Bible says to keep praying, so we're going to keep doing that too!'

This helped the boy enormously in his faith because, instead of being given a helpless position under an unpredictable God, he was rooted in the truth of who God is, what the Bible says about God, and how real relationship works with God in a situation like this.

Finding your child's view of God

Each child will have his or her own personal view of God. It is helpful for us to take a good look at our children's current view of God, and how they are responding to God, so that we know how to help each one of them move forward.

Your observations

Most of us have been watching our children their whole lives! What have you seen in your child's response to God? How does she talk about God? What questions does she ask? What is he like when you two pray together? You may want to create some opportunities for conversations about God just so that you can hear your child's ponderings about him. You can ask, 'What do you think God is doing today? How do you think God feels about... [something that is topical]? What do you think is God's favourite Bible story?' Since these questions don't have any 'right' answers, they free children to answer according to what they think and believe. If you can, just listen to their answers and ask more follow-up questions. If you feel comfortable with it, I would encourage you not always to try to correct any wayward thinking in that moment, as the most powerful part of this exercise is in releasing your children to talk about their real feelings about God. You will be creating a family culture in which the sharing of genuine thoughts and wonderings is valued above the performance of 'right' answers. Open questions will help you form an insight into your children's views of God without needing them to express those views directly.

Guided discussion

Guided discussion is another, more direct, activity that will help you to see how your children view God and how they feel about their relationship with him. Create a casual time in which you suggest to your family that you each draw a picture of what God looks like, where you are in the picture with God, and what your relationship with him feels like. Give some possible suggestions: for example, some people feel that God is a really busy man and they are in a bubble and can't hear God; or some people feel that God is a really old man on a cloud far away. They can draw anything. Coach your children along if they need it, asking for more detail on their drawing of God or for more specifics about how they feel connected to God (perhaps 'by a string', 'separated by a wall' and so on).

Don't let the children's drawings become pictures of the 'right' answer. If you feel they need reminding, emphasise that you want to know what they themselves think and feel. If you notice them slipping into performing for you, there is always the option of saying, 'Really? Because I wondered if maybe sometimes you felt that… [insert wise observation]. Many people feel that way sometimes. It's OK.' And don't forget to draw a picture yourself!

After the drawing time, share the pictures with each other and talk about them. Don't feel the need necessarily to solve any misconceptions at the time. Sometimes it is good to validate the sharing of our individual feelings about God, without needing immediately to correct or be corrected. This exercise is about taking a first step in helping children to own their relationship with God and in establishing the family as a great place to process your journeys with God. On the other hand, it might be a good time to discuss why we think in those ways about God and maybe start to unwind some wrong ideas. Only you will know what is right at the time.

Beginning to unwind

Once you know how your children view God, and have a better understanding of their relationships with him, you can begin proactively to unwind any unhelpful perceptions. There are many practical ways to do this, some of which we have already discussed; you will be able to come up with many more. Often, a key is to take another look at the child's ties between truth and experience and see if any repair work needs to be done. Each step is valuable, so don't feel you need to be in a rush. The process of unwinding unhelpful views and proactively rebuilding healthy ties of truth and relationship will begin to release your child to see God for who he truly is, and will empower him or her to crave a relationship with God.

Notes
1. Often the toilet is a good place for children to have some time out. You can't really send a seven-year-old on a walk, and not everybody has their own room at home. It also means that they can keep up the habit outside the home—at school, church or clubs—learning to exercise self-control through sharing with God and seeking his help and understanding.
2. Another aspect to look at is how we, as parents, respond to our child's failures and sins. Often, our responses can contribute to the way our children see God. If this interests you, Danny Silk has written a wonderful book called *Loving Our Children on Purpose* (Destiny Image, 2009), which helps us to model in our own parenting the freedom and consequences that God allows in his parenting of us.

*

— Chapter 5 —

Chatting with God

Five-year-old Laura snuggled into bed, having had her bath and bedtime story, and was ready for the final part of her routine—prayers. Her mother sat on the bed beside her and they settled into the pattern that happened every night. 'What do you want to pray about tonight?' Laura shrugged. 'I don't know.' Her mum sighed a little bit. 'Well, what should we say thank you to God for?' 'I don't know... for my hamster.' 'OK... what else?' Another shrug. Her mum tried again. 'It was very nice to see Nana and Grandad today, wasn't it? Maybe we should thank God for them?' Laura nodded. 'Is there anything you want to say sorry to God for?'

After a while, they managed to make it through listing some things Laura wanted to say sorry for and ask for, and the moment arrived for the prayer time. 'Would you like to pray?' 'Yes... umm no. You do it.' Her mum smiled. She couldn't remember the last time her daughter had prayed, but she always wanted to offer. 'OK, close your eyes. Dear God, thank you for Laura's hamster and for Nana and Grandad. Laura is sorry for hitting her brother and lying about it. Thank you for forgiving her. Please help her sore knee get better and help her friends to stop being mean to her at school. Amen.' 'Amen,' Laura replied. The bedtime routine complete, she put up her face for a kiss and a cuddle.

For many of us, this is an all-too-familiar dance that we do with our children at night or any time we attempt to get them to pray. Children who won't stop chattering all day can seem baffled by what to say when it comes to the time to pray. In some cases, we are happy if we just can get them to pray out loud for a sentence or two.

Everyone's experience with their children is different. Some children refuse to engage at all, so we pray for our children with blessings. Some children seem quite comfortable to rattle off a quick prayer, but the content seems to be lacking in personal connection.

In order to build a relationship with someone, we have to be able to talk with them. There has to be a willingness to share our thoughts and feelings with the other person, or it's not a relationship. So why do our children struggle to do this with God? Why is it so hard?

In the last chapter, we discussed how our children's views of God affect their reactions to him. Another major factor involved is the view of prayer that we have presented to them. Either intentionally or unintentionally, we may communicate to our children a definite set of 'rules' about prayer: what their bodies should do, what their words should say, and what content is acceptable. This set-up implies to our children that we can succeed or fail at how we perform the act of praying. That's a big pressure when the God of the universe is the audience!

As a tie-in, we may also present them with a style of prayer, both communal and private, that is distinctly one-way. It can be almost like leaving a message on God's answering machine, or like giving an important persuasive speech. We are the speakers and God is the audience. He likes listening; indeed, he is listening all the time. Any time we want to perform a prayer for him, he is ready to hear. We try to work on our children's skill in praying, teaching them how to think through ahead of time what they want to say and encouraging them to get better and better so that they can do it with confidence. We rejoice at the child who can pop off a prayer confidently and quickly, and we're impressed by his or her knowledge about God. The problem is that this type of communication isn't relationship- or connection-based at all. If we truly want our children to have a relationship with God, we need to readjust the way we shape their view of prayer.

The first step on that journey is to adjust our own approach. Many of us have cast ourselves in a role that we don't have—as a high priest. Before Jesus came to earth, Israel encountered God through a mediator, a high priest. This priest was super-impressive, super-holy and super-clean. He had the authority, power and awesome responsibility to speak to God for the people of Israel, bring God their sacrifices and make sure God was happy with all of them. He was also responsible for passing on God's words to the people, so that they could know his commands and encouragements—a bit like an ancient note-passer. The high priest was a very lucky man because he was the only person in the entire nation who was allowed to come directly into God's presence, in a room of the temple that no one else could enter, and only once a year. The Israelites had to experience God through him: their way of knowing God was through the words of the high priest. He mediated between them and God.[1]

When Jesus died on the cross, a significant thing happened in the Jerusalem temple. The veil separating the Most Holy Place, the room that was only for the high priest and God, from the rest of the temple was torn apart.[2] Jesus' death and resurrection changed for ever how people could encounter the living God. No longer were we reliant on someone to stand between us and God. Jesus made our sanctification possible so that we ourselves could encounter him daily, moment by moment.[3]

The trap we fall into is that we feel a need to stand between children and God, as if they still need a high priest to interpret God for them. See if any of the following statements ring true with you.

- My children won't really be able to understand prayer. I need to help them do it in manageable chunks.
- My child just doesn't know what to say, so I will do it for him until he becomes more confident.
- I don't want them to lose their reverence for God. I'm not convinced by the 'buddy Jesus' that so many people keep pushing. Aren't we called to fear the Lord?

- I just don't want my child to be disappointed with God. What if she prays and nothing happens? What if the thing she doesn't want to happen, does?
- I don't want my child to be hurt. What if all the other children hear God's voice and my child doesn't? I don't want my child to think God doesn't love him.

I'm not sure that this is a conscious, thought-out decision, but the desire to act like a high priest comes out clearly in our actions and words. When we pray with our children, we most often take the lead. Many times we will pray, instead of our child, if he or she is hesitant or uncomfortable. In our efforts to help, we create an overcontrolled environment where we feel it is safe for them to interact with God.

We help our children grow relationships all the time—with other children, teachers and family members. We help them develop their social skills. Most of the time, we put them in situations to learn for themselves, and we debrief them afterwards to help them grow. Toddlers don't fully understand the complexity of relationships, but, with a little bit of coaching and a lot of time in playgroups, they slowly figure out how to have as deep and emotional relationships as possible.

What if you insisted on sitting next to your toddler at every moment, speaking for him and interfering in his interactions with other toddlers and adults to prevent any confusion? If you did that, he would never learn how to build relationships for himself, communicate well or understand relational situations. He would be significantly hampered and isolated. We are constantly encouraging our children to take responsibility for their relationships, and we help them learn how to do them better. Why do we sometimes take a different approach in their relationships with God?

I find that this attitude comes mostly out of fear and distrust of God. On some level, perhaps a part of us believes that if God and our children interact unsupervised, the risk is high that they will be bewildered, hurt or somehow let down by who he is and what the reality of life with him is like.

It scared me so much when I saw that mindset in myself. In my passion for children to be close to God, I fell into the trap of fearing and distrusting God's very nature. I think we all need to face this question when we look at our role in parenting our children for relationship with him. Do I trust God? Do I know him well enough to be sure that he is a gentle God who reveals himself with faithfulness, patience and love? Do I trust that he knows my children better than I do, loves them more than I do and longs for a relationship with them more than I do? Do I trust that he created my child's mind, and that he can create a two-way communication with my child on her level in a way that is relevant to her?

Wanting children to have a safe place to encounter God is a right desire. My initial solution to that desire, though, was to put myself between God and children. I was the safety gate. Since I saw this tendency in myself, I've changed the boundaries. I don't want to be the safety gate between God and children. I want to be the steward—the one who guides a child into the presence of God and stands guard to protect their time and space as they interact. I want to be the one who walks with the child away from that encounter and helps him to process the way it changes his situation and life.

As we help our children to build that two-way connection with God, we need to periodically ask ourselves, 'Am I putting myself in the middle of this relationship, or am I functioning as a guide?'

Chatting

Children have been trapped in performance mode, and we need to give them an alternative way of interacting with God. Luckily, we have been provided with it! When Jesus was on earth, he lived side by side with his disciples. They were pioneers in a new way of interacting with God, a new way of 'praying'. When Jesus and the disciples woke up in the morning, I doubt that Peter wandered in for breakfast, noticed Jesus in the corner reading the morning news, said, 'Dear Jesus, please do not make us walk today. It is really hot. Amen,' and continued on his way. That would be rude. These men got to live with Jesus, who was fully God and fully man at the same time. They slept in the same house, ate food, laughed, debated and enjoyed themselves together. I can't say for certain, as the Bible isn't clear on this point, but I'm almost certain that they must have played some ancient version of 'I spy with my little eye' while on those long walking trips. In any case, they must have been bored together at some points, as well as being busy and serving alongside each other.

These people did real life with Jesus, and he shared his life with them. He asked for their support when he was upset and wanted company in Gethsemane. They knew when he was tired and wanted to go away and find some peace; they knew his moods and his habits. They talked back and forth with him. The Bible tells us that when we are forgiven, Jesus counts us as his friends, and God considers us his children.[4] We can interact with God as his close friend and his child. This is an intimate, everyday relationship that covers the whole range of experiences.

Our children would never interact with us the way they often interact with God, because they know that we want them to share everything with us and they know how they will be received. We can help our children to feel that same freedom and companionship in their relationship with God.

I use the word 'chat' with children when talking about prayer, because they tend to understand what it implies: an informal, about-anything, relational communication. When we break down the different aspects of chatting, we will see how easy it is to introduce it into our children's concept of relationship with God and guide them into using it every day. Each child's journey towards sharing his or her life with God is different, and will reflect each one's individual age, personality and way of doing relationship. There are four main areas we can look at to help our children connect with

God better—but remember, we don't have to work on all of these at once.

Using informal language

The way we talk to our friends and family is the most informal we can get. We don't worry about getting all of the words right; we just want to communicate however we can. Prayer, by contrast, has developed its own formal language that can get in the way when children want to communicate. It requires new words and even sentence structures that make it hard for children to talk to God with any spontaneity or real emotion: for example, 'Dear God, please bless Uncle David and Auntie Sue and Mummy and Daddy. Please forgive me for getting angry today at my little brother. Please watch over me as I sleep. Amen.' A child who isn't locked into this language may be able to communicate what she wants in such a way that she really feels she has connected to her Father God.

I was once doing bedtime prayers with a family friend's five-year-old daughter, and her chatted night-time prayer went: 'Hi, Father God! I had so much fun today, especially when I got to do girly stuff with Mummy when the boys were playing football. I don't know why you made football, anyway. It's silly. I had a bad part of the day when Tommy pushed me and I got really cross and smacked him. He makes me sad when he pushes me all the time. Can you make him stop being mean to me? I don't want to be mean either, but it's hard when he makes me cross. I'm going to sleep now. Will you please be in the room with me, 'cos I get scared sometimes. Oh, and please take care of Uncle David and Auntie Sue and Mummy and Daddy. I like them a lot. Love you!'

Help your child to feel free to use this sort of language by modelling how you do it. To start, try keeping your prayer times the same but, every time you pray, do it informally. This might be harder than it sounds: you might catch yourself quite a few times slipping in the odd 'bless' or 'forgive'. Take, for example, praying 'for the food' before dinner. Have you ever listened to what we say when we do this? Every once in a while, I still say, 'Bless this food to our bodies.' What does that mean? I'd much rather take the opportunity to pray, 'Thanks, God, for making sure we had the money to buy this food, and thank you for this family. I love them so much. Please join us right now as we spend some time together. We love you, God. Amen.'[5] The main thing to remember is that we want to train our children to communicate what is on their minds, in the way they want to, instead of trying to translate into a language that they feel is more acceptable to God.

Chatting about little things any time, anywhere

Communication with our family and friends is filled with half-spoken thoughts, ponderings, funny stories and really deep sharing. We often speak straight from the heart about what is going on with us, instead of thinking and planning what to say. In relationship, we share the little things in life because, eventually, big things will come along, and we need to know that the other person in that relationship cares about and can handle both.

Often, though, we encourage children to pray about the deep thoughts and feelings and ignore the little ones. There aren't many people we would do that with. The little things are important to children because life is made up of both big and small issues, and God longs to hear about all of it. Most children have been given a clear sense of what is 'proper' to talk to God about, but we can lift that lid off for them so that they feel the freedom of having a 'friend and family' connection with him. Everything is on the table: TV programmes, funny stories, how they feel about the colour of their underwear today, bodily functions, sports, anything and everything. Most children giggle and feel a bit shocked that God would care, but this way of praying brings them such freedom. I tell children, 'If it's in your head or heart, he wants to know!'

Modelling is key here. Most of us do this already in our lives:

we have informal running commentaries to God going on in our heads at many moments in our day, venting our frustration at God in the car park, thinking about our family situation or chatting to him about people on the way home from work. We do this while our children are talking or when we see an accident on the road that scares us, but children don't know that we do.

I have found that the most useful tool in modelling this kind of prayer is just to talk with children about what you do when you chat with God, and suggest that they try it. Most children just need their minds expanded to the possibilities. I tell them that my two favourite places to chat to God are in the shower or in the loo. I also say that I tell God jokes and chat to him while I watch TV. Whenever I'm lonely or scared, I start chatting to him right away about it. I love sharing life with him all the time. Many times, simply having this conversation can free children to try it for themselves.

You can also actively disciple your children in how to chat to God. Often, children need us to guide them through the process a couple of times before they will get the hang of it. Remember, we are trying to empower their relationship with God, and not put ourselves in the middle of it. So we can help to set up a situation for our children to try this kind of sharing with God. You can do this exercise as a family, or as part of your one-to-one time before your child goes to bed. After you have talked to your children about chatting to God and how he loves to hear about the little things in life, wait a short while and then have a go. Tell them that you are going to suggest something for them to tell God silently, and they can nod at you when they have finished. Once they nod, you can give another suggestion. This prayer is just between them and God, so I make sure they know that I don't want to hear the answer: they can tell God in their heads. (Children under six struggle with praying in their heads, so I often invite them to whisper their prayer into their hand or into their pillow, so that it's clearly between them and God, not them and me.) I structure the topics to interweave big and little issues so that they can experience a wide range of emotional sharing, side by side.

Some suggestions for what to pray about include the following. Tell or show God:

- Your favourite colour
- What you hope you are having for pudding tomorrow
- A joke
- The name of a person who hurts your feelings sometimes
- Which you would rather have for a pet: an elephant or a bear
- One thing you have to do every day that you wish you didn't have to do
- The best movie you have ever seen, and why you liked it so much
- One thing that you wish was different about your family
- Your favourite place in the whole world
- One thing you really like about yourself
- One thing that makes you super-scared
- How you feel about God: you can say anything!
- The person you are most glad that God created
- A time when you felt so lonely you wanted to cry
- One memory or picture in your head that you wish you didn't have
- The stinkiest smell you ever smelt

This list could go on and on. You would obviously tailor the questions to the age of your children, your family circumstances and the range of fun and deep things that you would like them to be sharing with God. This is a way of giving your children permission to talk to God about things at both ends of the scale: silly experiences, family situations, school bullying and so on. There is something very powerful about watching your child tell God a joke, with a giggle on his face, and then be given permission to tell God how he feels when Mummy and Daddy fight. A key in helping children to build a relationship with God is to show them that the connection with him is about everything, all of the time.

Sharing feelings, not just information

In order to simplify prayer, we often reduce it to an exercise in sharing information. If we want God-connected children, we need to help them create a pattern for sharing their thoughts and hearts. This is the essence of relationship—the ability to share our feelings with others. As children grow in their ability to recognise their emotions, they will grow in their ability to share them, and it is important that we make God a key person to share those emotions with.

You can learn to model this for your children by doing it in your own prayers: 'God, thank you so much for giving us another day together. I'm feeling really tired and a bit sad because I'm missing my husband Joe while he's on his trip. You have been helping me a lot every day, and I love feeling close to you. Thank you, too, for my son and daughter. They make my heart so happy and I love being their mum.' Learning to share feelings is a great way to become proactive in discipling children in their relationship with God.

Often, we train our children to pray at the end of the day as a catch-up, but chatting to God is a wonderful way of processing emotions while they are happening. God can handle being around us when we are angry or sad or irrational, so why not encourage your children to go for a walk in the garden and tell God how they feel when they are so annoyed that they want to scream? Or you might encourage them to find a secret place where they can share their hurt and sad feelings with God.

When working with older children, I often show them some key psalms. They are usually shocked by the emotions that the psalmists were 'allowed' to express to God. Take some time to find the right psalms to echo your children's emotions and experiences, and then encourage them to vent their frustration at God any time they want. If they like, they could also write their own psalms to God, expressing the way they feel.

Using non-verbal expression

Some children connect better with other ways of expressing themselves and sharing their thoughts and feelings with God. Some love drawing pictures of their feelings and experiences; others love journalling; some love choosing CD tracks of pop or worship songs that express how they feel, and playing them for God. Some children just need permission to share how they feel with a big growl or yell (obviously in some prearranged area where it is OK to make a noise). Some children need reminding that just inviting God to sit in a room with them while they are crying can be a way of sharing their feelings with God. You know your child best. Perhaps you could enable your children to try some of these different ways of expressing themselves to God.

Chatting is releasing

Chatting to God can release something wonderful in children because it frees them to be themselves and to share their lives with God. This allows their spiritual lives to pervade everyday experience. Whenever a family or community begins to explore this idea of chatting to God, I often hear stories of the impact it is having on children's lives. For example:

• A three-year-old's favourite thing to do is to play and chat with God in her room.

• Stewards at a summer conference reported that the loo and shower queues were longer than usual because the cubicles were taken up by children: their little voices could be heard, taking a 'private' opportunity to chatter away to God.

• A girl from a broken home who would rage with anger found that her best way to cope was to pour out her feelings to God instead of kicking and screaming at her parents.

- An older boy felt that all his feelings would get stored up inside him when he was bullied at school, and his hurt and shame and embarrassment would be like 'acid on my heart'. He found that chatting to God allowed all of those emotions to drain away.

Chatting with God is a key step for children in sharing their lives with God instead of performing for him. It is something that all of us long for in our lives, and we can help equip our children for the reality of this kind of relationship with God.

Notes
1. See Exodus 28:1—30:10; Leviticus 9:15–24; Leviticus 16; Hebrews 5:1; 9:7
2. Matthew 27:51
3. Hebrews 6:19; 10:19–22
4. John 15:15; Romans 8:15–17
5. A quick note on 'Amen': I tell children that we say 'Amen', which is just a fancy word for 'I agree', when there are lots of us praying together, so that each one of us can say, 'Oh yeah! I agree!' That's why we don't have to do it when we chat to God by ourselves. After all, we don't say, 'Please, Mum, can I have some milk. I agree with me!'

*

— Chapter 6 —

Catching God's voice

When I met Colin, he had been in two foster homes since being taken away from his family situation almost three years before. Eleven years old and recently adopted, he felt as if he had a 'volcano' of hurt and anger inside him. The smallest spark could set him off and, when it did, he lashed out at anyone around—screaming, kicking, punching and throwing things. After he'd exploded, he often crawled into his wardrobe and closed the door in an attempt to hide and feel safe. When the volcano erupted, he felt as if he couldn't stop it, and it often scared him to see 'who I really am inside'.

Veena and Ron, Colin's adoptive parents, had been actively modelling the reality of relationship with God at home and decided that they needed to be more proactive in creating opportunities for Colin to connect with God. I worked with them on how to help Colin hear God's voice, and they began to look for a chance to introduce the ideas to their son. One night, Colin talked about how his dad had always called him 'useless', and Ron felt that this might be a good opportunity to help Colin connect with God. He told Colin how God was really good at taking away bad things that people have said to us and replacing them with the truth. He offered to help Colin hear what God had to say about it. Colin hesitantly agreed, and Ron briefly outlined for Colin how to 'catch' God's voice. After a lightning-quick prayer from Ron inviting God to meet with him, Colin sat in silence, waiting, as Ron had told him, for God to do something. 'OK, God,' thought Colin, 'if I'm not useless, then what am I?'

Instantly, like writing on the inside of his mind, the word

'wonderful' appeared with little stars and fireworks exploding around it. Colin's eyes flung open and he whispered, 'He said something!' Ron asked about it excitedly while a smile lit Colin's face and warmth spread through his chest. 'Wonderful,' he said, out loud. 'Wonderful with fireworks.' Something broke in Colin and tears began to pour down his face. Quickly he shoved his face into his hands to hide it, and Ron gently asked if he could let God keep on talking to him. He nodded and, over the next couple of minutes, God and Colin met heart to heart—Colin chatting to God and God chatting back.

To be in relationship, communication must flow both ways. Not many of us would stay in a relationship where we were constantly doing all the communication and just had to guess how the other person was feeling and thinking. It's no fun chatting unless the other person chats back! God is faithful to communicate with us in a variety of ways, and we can train and equip our children to seek, expect and know his voice in their daily lives. It is an essential part of helping our children to have a relationship with him.

The Bible is full of God's promises that we will hear and know his voice. There are promises that he will speak to us when we call, and even when we don't. He speaks in different ways and gives us new and wonderful revelations. For example, he says, 'Call to me and I will answer you and tell you great and unsearchable things you do not know';[1] 'For God does speak—now one way, now another—though man may not perceive it.'[2]

God promises that we will grow to recognise his voice so well that we will run away from any other. For example:

'The man who enters by the gate is the shepherd of his sheep. The watchman opens the gate for him, and the sheep listen to his voice. He calls his own sheep by name and leads them out. When he has brought out all his own, he goes on ahead of them, and his sheep follow him because they know his voice. But they will never follow a stranger; in fact, they will run away from him because they do not recognise a stranger's voice.'[3]

God even promises that he will send his Holy Spirit to help us hear him clearly, and that the Holy Spirit will help us and guide us in this journey of understanding. For example:

'I have much more to say to you, but right now it would be more than you could understand. The Spirit shows what is true and will come and guide you into the full truth. The Spirit doesn't speak on his own. He will tell you only what he has heard from me, and he will let you know what is going to happen. The Spirit will bring glory to me by taking my message and telling it to you. Everything that the Father has is mine. That is why I have said that the Spirit takes my message and tells it to you.'[4]

Our lives can be full of God's voice and his communication. Many of us continually long for more of it in our lives, and we want our children to have a lifetime full of connection to God. So what is our role in connecting children to God's heart and voice?

The 'Eli calling'

When Jesus lived on earth, some people brought their children to see him. When the disciples tried to turn them away, Jesus insisted, 'Let the children come to me, and don't try to stop them!'[5] He didn't say, 'It is important for children to learn about me. Create some fab church programmes and a ten-step guide to teach children how to treat me correctly, and hopefully some will love me eventually.' He said, 'Let them come to me, and don't try to stop them.' Children, like all people, have a natural ability to encounter God and an innate desire to be with him.

I think that the real honour and privilege we have in our parenting of children might be described as an 'Eli calling'. Samuel was an Old Testament prophet who guided Saul as the king of Israel, and found and anointed King David. He was given to the temple of the Lord as a small child and was raised by a priest named Eli. Take a minute to read this story, paying particular attention to how Eli reacts to Samuel's experience with God. The story is from 1 Samuel 3:1–10 and 15–20.

Samuel served the Lord by helping Eli the priest, who was by that time almost blind. In those days, the Lord hardly ever spoke directly to people, and he did not appear to them in dreams very often. But one night, Eli was asleep in his room, and Samuel was sleeping on a mat near the sacred chest in the Lord's house.

(Everyone is in bed. Samuel is sleeping as close to God as he can get, right next to the high-priest-and-God-only room, the Most Holy Place. Eli is evidently in some other place, bedded down for the night.)

They had not been asleep very long when the Lord called out Samuel's name. 'Here I am!' Samuel answered. Then he ran to Eli and said, 'Here I am. What do you want?'

(My, what an obedient child! Or just one with a history of getting out of bed a lot? I love Eli's response. Since ancient times, the response to a child out of bed has always been the same.)

'I didn't call you,' Eli answered. 'Go back to bed.' Samuel went back. Again the Lord called out Samuel's name. Samuel got up and went to Eli. 'Here I am,' he said. 'What do you want?' Eli told him, 'Son, I didn't call you. Go back to sleep.'

(Notice the very good parenting style here: the firmer tone and the 'return' technique.)

The Lord had not spoken to Samuel before, and Samuel did not recognise the voice. When the Lord called out his name for the third time, Samuel went to Eli again and said, 'Here I am. What do you want?' Eli finally realised that it was the Lord who was speaking to Samuel. So he said, 'Go back and lie down! If someone speaks to you again, answer, "I'm listening, Lord. What do you want me to do?"' Once again Samuel went back and lay down. The Lord then stood beside Samuel and called out as he had done before, 'Samuel! Samuel!' 'I'm listening,' Samuel answered. 'What do you want me to do?' ...

(God told Samuel an important message: we are skipping ahead in the story a bit.)

The next morning, Samuel got up and opened the doors to the Lord's house. He was afraid to tell Eli what the Lord had said.

(It wasn't good news for Eli.)

But Eli told him, 'Samuel, my boy, come here!' 'Here I am,' Samuel answered. Eli said, 'What did God say to you? Tell me everything. I pray that God will punish you terribly if you don't tell me every word he said!' Samuel told Eli everything. Then Eli said, 'He is the Lord, and he will do what's right.' As Samuel grew up, the Lord helped him and made everything Samuel said come true. From the town of Dan in the north to the town of Beersheba in the south, everyone in the country knew that Samuel was truly the Lord's prophet.

I find it very powerful that God chose to speak to Samuel without being asked to, and it was Eli's role to point to God's already existing voice in Samuel's life. It was Eli's job to say, 'That is God speaking' and to guide Samuel in what to do when he heard God's voice. Eli trusted God enough and respected the child Samuel enough to let them interact with each other without feeling the need to control the conversation. (Remember that this was a time when it was rare to hear the Lord speaking.) Eli then debriefed Samuel after his experience (although I don't really recommend threatening the Lord's wrath if you can't get your child to talk!) and modelled how to submit to the word of the Lord with grace and honour.

This was a good spiritual parenting experience, but it could so easily have been missed. With a child out of bed three times in quick succession, Eli could have hit the roof, dragged Samuel back to bed and yelled, 'I *told* you to stay in bed, I am *not* calling you, *no* you can't have any water, and I *don't* want to see you up *again*!' Eli was tuned in enough to notice in the middle of the night that God was speaking to this child, to guide Samuel in how to respond, to keep himself out of the middle of the interaction and to debrief Samuel in the morning to talk about what had happened. Look at the fruit of this encounter in Samuel's life. God's call was established, a lifetime of blessing was begun, and his vocation was planted within him throughout the coming years, from one encounter with the Lord that Eli stewarded well.

God is calling each of us to a similar role. In order to help our children to connect with God and grow in relationship with him, we need to take Eli's lead and:

- Prepare our children for the ways God speaks.
- Identify in their lives the places where God is moving and validate their experience with him by guiding them forward in response.
- Debrief their experiences with them, helping them learn discernment to know what is and isn't God's voice.

- Proactively model and create new situations for them to grow in connection with God.

Preparing children for the ways God speaks

A big question that often pops up from people I work with is, 'What if God doesn't say anything to my child?' But we have seen in the Bible that God is talking—first one way, then another—and his plan is for us to know his voice. It isn't a question of trying to get God to speak. God is already speaking to our children; he is already blessing them, touching them, loving them. He is already giving them gifts, whispering in their ears, comforting them and forming them. Our children might just not be aware of it. Samuel didn't even know the Lord when God spoke to him: he couldn't recognise God's voice.[6] But God was persistent, and, with God's faithfulness and Eli's partnership in the intended encounter, Samuel's life changed for ever.

Catching God's voice

So how do we help children learn to recognise and know God's voice? In talking with children, I use the word 'catch' to mean perceiving God's voice, as it helps children to picture the approach we need. 'Prayer' brings with it all the connotations of restriction and one-way communication. 'Listening' implies that the process is ears-based only, so children can become fixated on 'hearing'. I use the word 'catch' because it implies a readiness and awareness to receive what God wants to communicate with all the tools we have at our disposal.

I explain it to children like this: when God made us, he made us for the whole purpose of hanging out with him, chatting with him, talking back and forth, and being in relationship with him. So that's how he made our bodies. He made our bodies to catch everything he wants to say to us and, because he is pretty clever, he doesn't just talk in words. He talks in a whole bunch of ways that our whole body can catch. When we catch, we need to be ready. It's really hard to catch when we're not looking. God's messages can pass by us unnoticed if we're not aware that he may be trying to communicate to us. Other times, we can forget to keep all our ways of catching ready. We can be so focused on one way that we miss how God is speaking to us. There are several main ways that we can 'catch' what God is saying to us.

With our brains[7]

- Pictures or movies in our minds: Take a second to close your eyes and picture your family. When we do this, we are not seeing people with our eyes; we are picturing them in our mind. That same place of picturing is a prime communicating area for God. We can use it to show God pictures of how we feel, our memories or hopes, or what has been happening in our day. He also loves dropping into that place pictures of his own that he wants to show us, movies of how he sees things, and his hopes and dreams and suggestions for us. Children can be very visual and creative, and God often meets with them in this way. Have some pens, coloured pencils and paper available for them to draw what God shows to them, so that they don't forget it and so that you can discuss it with them.

- Words in our mind: If we can sing in our heads or read a book quietly, we can identify that place in our heads where we can put words and 'hear' things without using our ears. We often chat to God by speaking only inside our heads, and he can chat back to that same place. Some children have full conversations with God, while others 'hear' only words or phrases. God can remind children of Bible verses they may have learnt, and he often gives them a Bible verse reference to look up, which they have never read before, so that he can continue to speak to them through his word. Again, having some paper and writing materials available helps children to solidify their experience in this area.

• Guided thoughts: Sometimes, when we are thinking a lot about things, solutions pop into our minds. Other times, in our ponderings we arrive at a place where we feel really, really good about what we have decided. God loves helping us to think about big questions and can participate in that process. This experience is slightly harder for children to identify, but, by their pre-teenage years, they can have begun to hear God's voice in their thinking and decision-making. For example, I was doing some work with pre-teenagers and teenagers in Switzerland, and we were outside spending some free time with God. The children were all over the side of a hill, writing, drawing, swinging, reading and doing whatever enabled them best to connect with God. I noticed that one girl kept staring at the facing hill with fierce determination. God pointed out to me two trees on the hill, isolated in the middle of a huge field, that I felt he wanted to speak to her about. I wandered over and casually said, 'Hey, have you noticed those two trees over there?' I got an excited smile. 'Yeah! God's been showing me them and telling me all about how we are like them.' God was not just dropping words in but guiding her thoughts and speaking to her about trees that had been planted many years ago.

With our ears and eyes[8]

Some children hear God's voice audibly sometimes, or see things that aren't there for everyone's eyes to see. I personally have never experienced this kind of communication but I have worked with adults and children who have. It can be a powerful and natural way of perceiving God.

With our skin[9]

The skin is the biggest organ in our body, so it makes sense that we can catch a lot from God with it. Common experiences when 'catching' with skin are feelings of warmth or tingles, a heavy head, or sometimes the feeling of a hand on the back. It's really important for children to understand that this is just one of the ways we can catch from God. Some people experience it often, and some people rarely do, just like all the other ways. I tend to avoid describing it in detail to children, as I never want to suggest to them what 'should' happen or encourage them to perform. I just let them know that they may catch in that way and watch what happens. When they describe to me their experience of catching with their skin, if it sounds right, then I validate it. One child new to catching from God complained that a big hand kept resting on his back while he lay on the ground and listened to God, but when we watched, we could confirm that no one was around him. Another four-year-old described to her mother that when she prayed before going to sleep, she felt God putting things into her hands. These are normal experiences that aren't to be overpraised or undervalidated. It is just another way that we can catch from God.

With our feelings or emotions[10]

God created emotions, too, and we can catch these from him if we are willing. Often, children who are ready to catch with their emotions can receive his peace, excitement, joy and sense of justice in wonderful ways.

With our guts[11]

This is just the feeling that you know that you know! Anyone who is open to catching from God can get a feeling of what God wants them to do, or a sense of the rightness or wrongness of a situation.

If children are playing a game that is a little dodgy, a child who is is open to God can often feel a strong sense that it is 'wrong' and decide not to participate. Other times, children may feel strongly that they need to pray for someone or ask someone a question. They can't necessarily tell you why, but they sense that God is nudging them in a certain direction.

In dreams[12]

God speaks in dreams, and our children can catch some great stuff from God while they sleep. Not every dream is from God, but, every once in a while, they will get a sense that maybe God was trying to tell them something in a dream. A notebook next to the bed can enable children to write their dreams down if they want to, so that you can discuss them together.

* * *

God speaks in different ways and, as individuals, we are all unique, catching better in some ways than in others. Eventually, we all develop our own patterns of how and when we catch God best. It is wonderful to see children develop in different ways: some connect with God best outside in nature, as God guides their thoughts of him; others love quiet and solitude inside as God shows them Bible verses, while others paint conversations with him in pictures. While it is good to encourage children to develop their preferences, it is also important that we keep presenting them with new options and new experiences, training them to stay open to every way of perceiving God, so they don't miss anything that God has for them.

'What happens if children don't "catch"? I don't want my child to feel left out or ignored by God. I don't want him to feel hurt and then walk away from his faith.' This is a question that I get asked whenever I speak at an event. First of all, I want to say that it is an understandable question. Each one of us has had a specific, unique journey and relationship with God. We have experiences that we cherish in our lives with him, and we all have questions, doubts and struggles. Somewhere along the road, some of us have been wounded or felt that God has let us down, specifically with regard to hearing God speak. Many of us have felt the sting of longing to hear God's voice at a particular moment in time, and finding that it didn't happen. This experience may have significantly shaken our faith, or it may not even have surprised us.

The problem is that sometimes we pass on those questions, doubts and struggles to our children as truth, in our words, advice and guidance. We let them attach to our children and then feel hurt for them as they struggle under the weight of our difficulties. My view is that learning how to live in relationship with God is not as easy as we would like to make it for children. We are all on a journey of relationship, learning to hear and access God's voice in our lives. We are on the journey, and our children are on the journey. To say that we want our child's journey of connection to God to be always uncomplicated and successful is unrealistic, and doesn't serve them well. Our privilege is to help them learn how to walk this relational path with God, not hide it from them. We get to walk with them through joy and success and struggle. We get to shape their experiences for them, so that they can view their 'disappointments' with a godly and connected approach.

Will there be times when your child doesn't 'catch' God? Yes, absolutely. That is the reality of living as imperfect people in a broken world. But the goal isn't to catch God; the goal is to connect with him, and we can teach children how to handle all aspects of that connection. When a child is struggling to 'catch', I validate that experience as well. I say, 'That's OK; I sometimes find it hard, too. Sometimes my brain is too busy or my heart is too loud, or sometimes I just can't connect. But we do know that God loves us, is talking to us and wants us to know his voice. So we'll keep being open to him. Why don't you tell God how you feel about it? Sometimes I feel cross or sad, or both. Why don't you tell him?'

Identify, validate and guide into response

I firmly believe that God is already talking to our children, and it is our job to help them identify where. We have been given the opportunity to direct their attention to their lives and say, 'Look! That's God!' Sometimes God speaks clearly to them without their being briefed for the experience at all. Once children open up to the possibility that God may speak to them and they begin to understand and experience his doing so, it can happen at any time—in the back of the car, at school, at bedtime or while they sleep.

At some moments, as he did with Samuel, God speaks to our children and they come to us in the middle of an exchange with him. Often, this happens when children unexpectedly become aware that God may have spoken to them out of the blue or in response to their questions. Children can be so shocked to catch God speaking that they completely disengage from the experience to come and tell us. These are the times when children need us to help them identify God's voice, validate their experience and guide them to know what to do next. It is important that we celebrate with them when this happens, but the goal for their lives isn't to manage to hear his voice, but to engage in relationship with him.

We need to be overjoyed for our children that they and God are meeting up, and we need to give them suggestions for what to do next. Most of the time, we may simply need to guide them to reconnect with God, so they can finish the encounter that they or he started. Sometimes, children just need validation to feel encouraged to go back to their encounter. Sometimes, like Samuel, they need more directed suggestions for how to respond.

A good approach is to ask your child a natural follow-up question. One mum in my church told me a story of her nine-year-old daughter, Natalie. She was sitting in the back seat of the car while her mum drove. All of a sudden, she gasped and said, 'I was just thinking about school and my friends, and God showed me a picture of a dolphin jumping and diving in the sea!' 'That's great, sweetie! Why do you think he showed you that picture?' asked her mum. 'I don't know!' Natalie replied and picked up her book to start reading. 'Well, why don't you ask him?' her mum suggested. 'Um, OK!' Natalie put the book down and looked out of the window, reconnecting with God. After a few seconds, she piped up, 'He said that my heart was the sea and he was the dolphin, and he was going to dive in and play with me in my heart. Really close and fun-like.' Natalie smiled broadly. Natalie's mum had been able very gently to turn her child back to God to complete the conversation that God had started, just by asking a question and nudging her back to the place of receiving.

One four-year-old boy, Jonathan, told his mother about two dreams he'd had on two successive days, which he thought were from God. The first day, he said, he and Jesus were on a donkey going to Jerusalem. They were having a great time, singing songs and laughing. Then they came to a river and Jonathan said, 'Jesus, what is that?' Jesus said, 'It's me! Any time you are sad or lonely, you can drink it and I'll be with you!' His mother's jaw dropped and everything in her wanted to launch into a three-point explanation of the significance of the symbolism of water and Jesus, but one look at his face stopped her. Jesus had revealed a part of himself to Jonathan, and it was perfect for him. She just said, 'Yep, that sounds like a dream from God to me.' His little face scrunched up as he nodded, 'I think so, too.' She nodded with him. 'Sounds like you are catching some good things from God in your dreams. I'm looking forward to hearing about any more you think God might want to give you.'

The next day, Jonathan came back to her. He suffered quite badly from nightmares and had recently been up for significant portions of the night, several nights a week. Jonathan said that he'd had another dream in which he and Jesus were back on the donkey, heading for Jerusalem. A lot of black scary monsters ran towards them, trying to attack and pull Jonathan off the donkey.

Jonathan was very scared but Jesus said, 'Don't be scared. I have given you some of my power. Tell them to go away because I said so.' Jonathan said 'OK', squinted his eyes, put his hand out in a stop sign and said very loudly, 'You guys go away because of Jesus.' Instantly, the black scary monsters screamed and went away. His mother confirmed to him that it seemed that God had given him a great dream with some good advice, and that if he ever had another nightmare he should do what Jesus told him to do.

Jonathan's mum reported to me weeks later that, occasionally, she still hears her son squeak out in the middle of the night: 'Go away because of Jesus' power inside me.' When she goes to check on him, he's snuggled in bed with a smile on his face and sleeps through the rest of the night, undisturbed. She can see the fruit of her 'Eli calling' night after night in her son's sleep.

Debrief and discern

The morning after God had spoken to Samuel, Eli made sure he asked what God had said. We are the mature and wise people whom God has placed in our children's lives to help them process their encounters with him. We are also the people whose job it is to help them learn to recognise God's voice. It is so amazing to hear our children tell us of their encounters with God and how they are doing in their relationship with him. We can help to guide their thinking and ask crucial questions that make them think hard about how those conversations with God affect the choices in their lives.

It is also our job, though, to make sure our children have the skills to recognise when the voice they hear is not from God and to know what to do about it. This responsibility terrifies many people, and I understand their concern. We don't want our children running around thinking every thought that pops into their head is from God. But, for many of us, this means that we have shied away from wanting our children to connect with God, for fear of opening the 'floodgates of ambiguity', as one parent put it.

I am not scared by this, as I see part of my job as helping my child learn to distinguish God's voice. Remember the passage in John that talks about the shepherd leading his sheep? 'His sheep follow him because they know his voice. But they will never follow a stranger; in fact, they will run away from him because they do not recognise a stranger's voice.'[13] Connecting to God involves a process of learning to recognise God's voice, so that eventually we know it so well that we can boldly reject any other voice that tries to pass as his. If I called to your children, they would probably ignore me or stay away from me, even if I used their names. When you call your children, though, they recognise your voice because, over the years of their lives, they have become attuned to it (even if they pretend not to hear!). They will learn to recognise God's voice only by perceiving it over and over again, with you helping them to identify and affirm it accurately. The more they experience it, the more they will know it and begin to recognise it on their own.

Children need to learn how to take what they 'catch' and make sure that it is from God. This is a relatively easy process of matching what they hear to what we know about him from the Bible. Children do this kind of thing all the time in their everyday lives. For example, let's assume you have always told your children that they can never drink blackcurrant squash in the living room. Their world will end if they drink blackcurrant squash in the living room; all their privileges will grind to a halt if they drink blackcurrant squash in the living room. It has been like this for their whole lives. What would happen if I came over to your house and said, 'Hey, let's take this blackcurrant squash into the living room and drink it on your parents' white sofa. Your parents said it would be all right'? There is no way they would believe me. It has nothing to do with me: they know *you*, and there is no way *you* would say that. Anything that they perceive in their encounter with God has to be held up to the same sort of standard.

This is one of the times when it helps to be both God-smart and God-connected! If your six-year-old child is chatting to God after putting in a terrible performance at her flute recital, and if she feels rubbish and thinks that God thinks she should give up the flute because she will never be any good, you can help her hold that experience up to God's character and his word. 'Hmmmm, I'm not sure that sounds like something God would say. Let's see. We know that God loves us and loves to be involved with us. We also know that his voice brings us encouragement and joy. It sounds as if you feel hurt and put down by those words. I don't think that was God at all. I think we can throw those words away. They don't get to stay in your head.'

It's important that we don't just help children to discern God's voice, but also teach them what to do, when they are tuning in to God, with thoughts that aren't from him. Any thoughts that are potentially damaging to themselves or other people don't get to stay in their heads. I explain to children that they can put those negative words or pictures in a box in their head and shrink it until the box disappears, because God doesn't want us to let those thoughts hang around. God only wants us to have positive ideas in our minds.[14]

Children of all ages can understand this concept well. Why not take some time with your children to make a chart that has 'From God' and 'Not from God' written at the top? You can make up all sorts of silly thoughts and your children can put them in the right categories, so that they learn ahead of time how to identify what is from God and what isn't.

Tying together truth and experience

Our children's encounters with God are powerful to them and influence the way they live their lives. This is one of the key areas where biblical truth and relational experience with God need to be inextricably tied together, but what does that mean in practice?

Catching from God is like all other types of experiences with him. It needs to be rooted in truth, so that children can see the Bible in their experience and their experience in the Bible. This doesn't mean, though, that every time our children hear from God we need to take out our Bibles and make them find a relevant verse in there. That would stifle the very thing we want to create in our children—the knowledge of how to operate in a fluid and personal relationship with God. Rooting in the Bible is vital but we need to help children to discern spiritually in the same way we help them to discern in other areas of life.

- First, we build a foundation of knowledge out of which they can operate. In everyday life, this means teaching them to tell right from wrong, what we expect of them, how to conduct themselves in any situation—an endless list that we build into our children to establish their worldview. We will be doing the same thing with our children spiritually, building in them a biblical foundation of who God is, what his word says, and how our relationship with him is designed to work. The result is that our children will be able to recognise the character of God and the truth of his word in what they hear when they meet with him.
- At times when they are wrong or unsure, we help them search out the answer. In ordinary life, we debrief with them, ask them guiding questions, challenge them if necessary and, at important moments, sometimes say straight out that we think they may be wrong. We will be doing the same thing with our children spiritually. If they encounter something in their experiences with God that makes them feel unsure, or that we feel is wrong, we can pursue it with them, to train them how to spot wrong thoughts and be sure about them. We may bring the Bible out to research more into who God is and what he says, so that they can measure their experience against his word. This is a continual process of teaching them how to develop deeper roots and measure their life by a standard.

- At times of success, we affirm them in their choices. In everyday life, we tell them how proud we are of them, compare their bravery or strength to other model people we know, and explain how we see their choices reflected in the foundations that they have built. We will be doing the same thing with them spiritually. As they share their experiences with God with us, we can affirm for them how we see God reflected in what they say and in the fruit it has been bearing in their lives. We can tell them biblical stories that affirm their experiences and show them Bible verses that echo what God has been saying and the way he has been saying it.

Proactively model and create

Modelling

We are perfectly positioned to model to our children how to 'catch' God's voice. God has placed our children in our homes so that we can walk with them as we go on our individual faith journeys. They are like sponges, watching us and soaking up what they see as we pioneer the journey ahead of them, so we need to provide a framework from which they can deal with any spiritual issue that heads their way.

Children need to see us engaging in this aspect of relationship with God. They need to see how we do it and what impact it has on us. We need to remember to create windows into our experiences of catching from God. If you keep a journal, you could show your children some pages that you feel are appropriate to share, once in a while. Talk about how God's voice has influenced the way you feel about current situations or helped to shape your decisions. Take Bible verses that God has used to encourage you and stick them on your mirror, so that your children can see how to use God's words to remind them of his truth. Invite them to catch what God has to say to you. In my prayer journal, I have several handwritten notes and drawings that children in my church have received from God to pass to me. I cherish them very much, and so do the children.

Create new opportunities to connect

At the end of the story of Eli and Samuel, we see the fruit of their encounter with God. The Lord is with Samuel as he grows up and eventually becomes universally hailed as a mighty prophet of God. To me, this implies that there were many more encounters as Samuel grew in his relationship with God and his ability to identify and discern God's voice. We, too, need to be continually looking at how to encourage our children to step into these encounters again and again. Remember, these are individual times of building a relationship with God that you can help your children to identify—a bit like setting times for friends to come home to play or scheduling visits. Eventually, the goal is for your children to handle all of that themselves, but, until they do, you can help.

- Journal: Many children love the tangibility of a journal. In it they can record conversations they have with God (a common practice), pictures from God or to God, things God says, memories that God reminds them of, letters to God and so on. It also gives children a record of God's encounters with them for those wobbly days that all of us have, when we are convinced that God never speaks to us. They will have a whole book to prove otherwise.
- Bedtimes: This is a great time to create space for your children to hear from God. You can build into the bedtime routine a two- to ten-minute span when you play worship music and your children chat and catch with God or write in their journals.
- Family times or family decisions: If a family decision is coming up, you could try asking the whole family to spend some time catching from God about it. Then everyone can come together as a family and discuss what God is saying to you all.

- **Reading a story:** This is a fantastic way of helping children engage with God. Take a good quality children's book and, when you have finished reading it to your children, suggest a question to ask God and catch his answer. For example, Max Lucado's book *You are Special*[15] is about a wooden man named Punchinello who lives in a town where the inhabitants give shiny stars and black dots to praise and tear down each other. Punchinello eventually learns that it doesn't matter what the other people say; it is what his master thinks about him that counts. The more he cares about his master's view of him, the less those stars and dots stick to him. At the end, it would be very easy to say, 'Sometimes we all feel worried about what other people say about us, but it is more important to know what God thinks about us. Why don't we ask him?' Take some space for you both to catch from God what he says, and discuss it.
- **Asking questions:** Sometimes children need to be helped to see when a question would be a good one to take to God. The Bible says that the Holy Spirit will guide us into all truth,[16] so we should encourage our children to feel free to ask God anything they want. 'Sounds like a good thing to ask God' can become a standard phrase in your house.

These opportunities to connect with God will be original and personal to each of your children. Every child is different, and you will be able to create what each of your children needs, based on how well you know them. I'd like to share a story about a family I knew who did this really well. In the introduction to this book, I told you about Richard and Jill and their daughter, Lily. If you remember, Lily grew up in the church but struggled with confidence and life issues.

Lily's parents attended a course about how to influence and guide their children's faith as parents, and they began proactively to help Lily process her days with God in mind. They watched, waited and prayed while they chose to guide conversations towards the ways God might have direct input into her situation. They created times to encounter God individually while still together in the same space, one day having a catching time together in the afternoon, another day playing loud worship music and singing while cooking. Another day they enjoyed journalling together, sitting and listening to the fire crackle. They created a daily 'question to ask God' board that gave new ideas of questions to ask during the day, and then they discussed their experiences with God at dinner time. They tried to show Lily the myriad different ways in which God and life happen together. Lily began to learn what God's voice sounded and felt like, and wanted more of those experiences in her life.

Gradually, Lily learned how she liked to connect with God best. She loved being on her own in a little hiding place in the quiet. She loved writing down what she felt God was doing in her life and what he was saying to her. Lily's parents were on hand to facilitate her next step. They helped her design a little corner of her room to be her secret space. They got her some pillows and a blanket, a journal, a Bible, some pens and some Post-it notes. Every night, before she crawled into bed for their normal routine, Lily would go into her corner to spend time with God, reading the Bible, chatting and catching. Sometimes Richard or Jill would get invited into the corner; some nights it was just Lily and God.

Her journal began to fill with little sentences. 'God says I am beautiful, and he really likes my forehead freckle. He put it there on purpose.' 'God says I am great at helping people and have a big heart like the Grinch.' (I assume, after it got three times bigger.) 'God showed me a picture of the bad words stuck in my head, written on a whiteboard. He showed me that he will wipe those words away any time I ask him to, if people write bad stuff on it that I don't like.' She also wrote down what she and God did together: 'I asked God to fix the hurt in my heart, and my head got heavy and I felt all tingly and quiet inside my tummy. I didn't cry about it after that; it felt all better.' The walls of her corner filled with Post-it notes to remind her of the prayer requests that she wanted to pray about every day. She put up colourful handmade posters of her favourite Bible promises and illustrated them with pictures that showed what they meant to her in her life. In her catching from God, Lily discovered that she was good at helping people, so she announced to the leaders of the crèche that she had the helping gift and that she would now be helping them set up and take down the equipment each Sunday. She would even wrangle and organise other children to help as she served faithfully each week.

Lily's confidence and peace have grown immensely since her parents showed her how to connect with God. They continue to encourage her, resource her, monitor her and guide her as she learns how to live life connected heart-to-heart with God.

Notes
1. Jeremiah 33:3 (NIV)
2. Job 33:14 (NIV)
3. John 10:2–5 (NIV)
4. John 16:12–15
5. Matthew 19:14
6. 1 Samuel 3:7
7. Acts 2:17–18; 9:10; Joel 2:28
8. 2 Kings 6:10–17; Acts 7:54–56
9. 1 Kings 8:10–11
10. John 14:27; Philippians 4:7; 1 Peter 1:8
11. 1 Corinthians 12:8; John 4:1–9
12. Genesis 20:3; Matthew 2:13; Job 33:14–18
13. John 10:4–5 (NIV)
14. Philippians 4:8
15. Max Lucado, *You are Special* (Crossway, 1997)
16. John 16:13

*

— Chapter 7 —

Praying with children

We had just finished the funeral in the back garden. Her older brothers had quickly run off to continue playing, but Alice was still beside herself with grief. At eight years old, it was her first experience of death, and she was taking it quite hard, especially as it was such a close friend who died—her pet gerbil, Wonder. I saw her run up the stairs to her room. Her father, Kevin, followed her up and sat down next to her as she curled on her bed, looking woefully at the empty cage on the desk opposite. They had had many discussions over the last day about death and sadness, but Alice still seemed to be experiencing a lot of conflict.

Kevin decided that Alice needed some help processing her grief, and he thought that connecting with God about it might enable her to begin to move on. Kevin gently suggested to Alice that he would like to help her have a chat with God about what had happened and how she was feeling. 'Oh yes, Daddy, please,' she replied. 'Could you ask God to help Wonder have a good time in heaven?' Tears welled up in her eyes. Kevin thought, 'Help a dead gerbil have a good time in heaven? This is going to be interesting.' Kevin smiled at his daughter. 'OK, darling, I'm going to chat to God a little bit, and then I'm going to stop and we are going to be quiet for a while. While we are being quiet, you can chat to God about how you feel, and I want you to wait and catch with your whole body what God wants to give you. After a while, I'll check on you to see how it's going, OK?' Alice sniffled, 'OK, Daddy.'

Kevin put his big hand lightly on her back while Alice closed her eyes, as she liked to do whenever she caught from God. 'Father God, you love us so much. God, Alice is feeling very sad and her heart hurts very much because Wonder died. He was such a fantastic friend to Alice, and she is feeling scared about what life will be like without him. Please come and speak to her.' He paused. 'Now let's wait.' Seconds and minutes ticked by while he watched his daughter's face as she connected with God, and he saw her body relax. He could sense that she was chatting to God and that he was connecting back.

After about two minutes, Kevin felt it was right to check on how she was doing, so he asked gently, 'How's it going? What has God been doing?' She opened her eyes and smiled a little. 'He feels sad for me. He said that Wonder was a gift he gave me and that he will give me more gifts like that—friends and things that help me feel safe inside and happy inside. He showed me a picture of him sitting in my room with me when I get lonely and think of how much I miss Wonder. I feel quieter. It's nice.' Kevin smiled. 'Good, I'm glad. Do you want to spend more time with God, or have you finished?' Alice shrugged. 'I've finished.' 'Do you want to write down what God said or draw the picture in your journal?' 'Yes, but not right now. I'm going to go and play with James and Pete.' As Alice ran down the stairs, Kevin breathed a sigh of relief and thanked God for his faithfulness to minister to the broken-hearted.

In the last chapter, we discussed how to train and empower children to build a relationship with God by catching his voice in their daily lives, with very little involvement on our part in the actual encounters. Sometimes, though, there are circumstances in which our involvement is very helpful. There are times in all of our lives when situations are overwhelming or it is very difficult to see a way out of them. We may feel trapped in our feelings, locked into a corner or just pushed down by others. Often, in specific times of grief, hurt, bullying, difficult family situations or intense social conflicts, our children need our proactive intervention to help them connect with God, just to get the ball rolling and to reopen that area for them in their lives. If you see your children looking lost, struggling to connect with God or lacking confidence in themselves, it might help to offer to pray with them.

Our approach to praying with our children will be slightly different from the situation we discussed in the previous chapter: this time, we are playing an active role in the encounter with God, while still ensuring that we are not in the middle of it. Our main role in these situations is to connect our children to God in a way that empowers their relationship and doesn't make them dependent on us to continue the connection.

It is a very simple model that ensures consistency with all we have been teaching them about connection to God, but still places us in a position of influence and assistance. I will explain the model and then include a few stories so that you can see how it works out in different situations.

Understand

As always, it helps if we can get a good handle on what the issue really is. I have made so many mistakes by assuming that I know what the problem is or by minimising the issue, instead of taking an extra ten seconds to make sure I really hear what is being said.

Explain

Take a couple of seconds to explain what is going to happen. Adults may have people praying with them all the time, but for children it can be a new experience. For the first few times, it really helps to let the child know how it is going to go. Children find safety in knowing what you are going to do, what God is going to do, and what you expect them to do. They especially need to be told how they will know when it's over.

I often ask children to close their eyes and hold their hands out loosely in front of them as if they were ready to receive a gift from someone. For many children, this helps them to be aware of and open to what God is doing.

Touch

Touching our children while we pray together is natural and biblical. It helps them know that you are there and not going away, and it empowers them to feel braver in opening themselves up to what God wants to do with them. I find that a simple light hand on the shoulder does the trick. If the hand is too heavy or moves around, it can distract the other person from their connection with God, so make sure your child is comfortable.

Pray

The purpose of the prayer isn't mainly to pray for our child, but to guide them to God so that they can meet with him. This can be a hard thing to do, because we love praying for our children and we love talking a lot when we pray. Our children don't need us to speak to God for them, though; they need us to help bring them to God so that they can talk between themselves. If we fall into the trap of praying in long and complicated sentences, we can communicate to our children that the way we pray is important, and that we are much better at it than they are. They may begin to become dependent on our prayers, instead of feeling empowered in their own connection. We will be most effective if we focus on a few guidelines.

- Instead of repeating the facts of the situation, communicate to God the heart of the matter. In the case of the dead gerbil, Alice mainly wanted God to help her gerbil have a good time in heaven. The heart of the matter was that Alice was hurting and scared, so that is what her father brought to God.
- Keep your prayer to three or four simple sentences. This helps the child to stay engaged and focused on the coming encounter instead of being bored and disengaged because we are doing the praying for them. Even if the child's house blew down, his

cat is missing, his school hours have extended until eight in the evening and all of his friends have decided they like girls and won't play with him any more, we can still reduce our prayer to three sentences. (I would suggest, 'Father God, Joey's life is going crazy right now, and he is feeling all sorts of feelings. He feels lost and angry and sad, and he really needs your help. Please come now and calm the storm in his heart and mind so that he and you can meet and you can give him what he needs to make it through.') It is worth practising this in advance: when issues arise in your child's life, think 'How would I pray about this in three sentences?' so that you are ready with the skills when you need them.

- Try to keep the invitation vague at the end. When I ask God to minister to children, I try to stay as open as possible to what God wants to do. It would have been very easy for Kevin to ask God to bring peace and comfort to his daughter Alice, but this would have influenced Alice to be expecting only those gifts from God. Instead, Alice got something very different. There are definitely circumstances where specific requests are helpful, and we should feel free to ask for specific things from God, but, as a general principle, I try to stay open. God knows what my child needs much better than I do.

- Don't say 'Amen'. Often, children hear 'Amen' as 'The end' and disengage. I just remind the child, 'Now let's wait while you and God chat and catch with each other. I'll check on you in a bit.'

Wait

Waiting can be the hardest part of the prayer for us, as we have no control over anything but ourselves in the deafening silence. This is when our faith truly goes on the line, because we tell our children, 'Now you and God get to meet', and we have to trust that God is faithful to be there. Everything in us is screaming, *'God, you'd better be here speaking to my child and giving him what he needs because this child is so precious to me and I want him to know you, so don't you disappoint him. Now, God, speak now!'* while we keep calm and confident smiles on our faces, waiting and watching.

Knowing our tendency to rush this part of prayer, I would encourage you to wait for an average of 30 seconds before moving on. That's 30 real-life seconds, not counting to 30 as fast as you can! Another good measure is to wait as long as you can bear, then wait ten seconds more. At first, we think 'My child will never sit still that long', but that is only because we have never seen them wait in prayer or because we haven't trained them to do so. If a child's eyes pop open before the minimum time is up, I often say, 'Not yet; let's wait a bit more so that you can catch from God.' My minimum waiting times tend to be ten seconds for children up to five years old, 30 seconds for 5–7s, and between 30 seconds and one minute for children over eight. Having said that, I've seen under-fives waiting for ten minutes, 5–7s having a blast with God for 15 minutes, and nine-year-olds out for 45 minutes to an hour, so there really is no hard-and-fast rule. My 30-second guideline is meant more for those of us who tend to rush than for the children who are meeting with God.

It is important that we keep our eyes open and watch our child to see how they are doing, but try not to read too much into what we see. Adults become adept at showing other people how they are feeling when they pray, but children are often without that device. 'Bored' often looks the same as 'having an amazing encounter with God', so just trust that God is speaking. Feel free to pray silently for your child while he or she is meeting with God, while keeping track of time.

Check

When you feel it is right, quietly ask your child an open-ended question such as 'How is it going?' 'How are you feeling?' or 'What has God been doing?' Checking in this way is often harder than we think, as our brains may freeze and we end up asking 'Did God say anything?' or 'What did you catch?' These sorts of questions may imply that either God or our children might fail. Open-ended questions allow our children to process their experience, no matter what it was.

It's possible that we may interrupt a good conversation or experience that the child hasn't finished yet and may want to get back to. (I have been told by numerous children when I checked in on them, 'Shhh, you're interrupting God' or 'We're busy!') If, in response to your question, you get 'Good' or 'He's helping me', I would suggest you say, 'Great! You keep going with God as long as you want!' Then wait for a significant time longer—until you are pretty sure they have finished. Children need to know that we want them to spend as much time as they like with God; they should feel no time pressure from us at all.

If a child seems eager to talk, this would be a good time to debrief. It is also the time to affirm them and help them with discernment if they are struggling. Sometimes a child will answer, 'I don't know' or 'Fine'. That's not a negative answer; nor is it a cop-out. It just means that they haven't fully worked out what has just happened. I would encourage you to ask some follow-up questions to allow them to process their experience out loud: 'Tell me more about it'; 'What happened when we went quiet and waited?' 'What did you feel like?' These questions may help them to replay the experience in their head.

Offer

After we have finished checking in and debriefing, it is important that we invite the child to go back and spend more time with God. Often, a response to being with God is to want to spend more time with him or to connect with him about issues that are more specific. Be willing to stay and help the child reconnect, or leave them to sit and catch more from God. Suggest things that you feel are appropriate for them to do as a follow-on from their experience—for instance, writing in a journal or drawing what God showed them, chatting and catching with God later on their own, or coming to you for help to connect with God again.

As I have said, this is a simple model that will become more streamlined, the more you do it and the more your children become familiar with the process. Eventually, it will equip them to seek God for the deeper, more complicated issues that arise in their lives.

Examples

Let's look at some more real-life examples of parents who have prayed with their children, to see the model in action.

Charlie shifted uncomfortably in his seat, his feet tapping nervously on the floor. Charlie's dad, Jon, leaned over to check on how his seven-year-old son was doing. Charlie had two more performances to watch before his turn, and he was desperately uneasy. 'You OK?' Jon whispered quietly into his son's ear. Charlie kept looking at the floor and nodded. 'You want me to pray with you?' Charlie's eyes stayed on the floor as he emphatically nodded. 'OK. I'll pray and then we'll be quiet for a bit so that God can meet with you, and then I'll check and see how you're doing. I promise that you'll have plenty of time to get ready for your turn, OK? I'll watch the performances, trust me. Just you-and-God time now. OK?'

Charlie took a shaky sigh and nodded slowly. Jon lightly put his hand on his son's tiny shoulders as Charlie tilted his hands up and closed his eyes. 'Father God, thank you for all the gifts and character you have given to my son. He is nervous and wants to do well today in his performance. Please come and meet with him right now and pour into him all he needs to be himself and do well.' Charlie's feet stopped tapping and his head dropped a little as Jon watched God pour peace and confidence into his son. A performance piece ended and Charlie's head began to come up, but Jon quickly whispered, 'Plenty of time' and Charlie settled back into catching from God. When it was time, Jon squeezed his son: 'How are you feeling now?' Charlie's eyes met his dad's with a relieved smile. 'Good.'

'What was God doing?'

'Made me stop feeling jittery in my hands and my insides and told me that he is excited to hear me play. He knows how much I like it, and he likes it, too.'

Jon smiled. 'He certainly gave you a gift for it!' he said.

* ✱ *

A scream punctured the air, and Helen ran into her three-year-old daughter's room. She found Amelia on the floor, clutching a bleeding knee that had just taken the brunt of an awkward fall on to a sharp toy. Slightly relieved at the small size of the cut, Helen compassionately swept her daughter into the bathroom to wash and cleanse it. Clearly shaken up, Amelia was still crying and shivering, and Helen realised that the actual fall must have been scarier than its consequences. Helen offered to pray with Amelia and cuddled close as she accepted.

Helen explained quickly that she was going to chat to God and then they were both going to wait to catch what God wanted to say or give to Amelia. Then Helen would check to see what God had been doing. Amelia's little head nodded against her mother's chest as Helen got comfortable. 'Father God, Amelia got very scared by her fall. Her body is all shaky and hurt. Please come and chat to Amelia and give her everything she needs to feel better.' Helen dropped her voice to a whisper: 'Let's wait and see what God does! Don't forget to catch with your whole body!' Amelia's shaking stopped and her breathing slowed as they waited in silence on the floor of the bathroom. After 30 seconds or so, Helen asked, 'What is God doing?' Amelia smiled, 'I'm catching with my skin! He's putting water on me to cool me down!' Helen smiled back, 'Oh, good. I'm glad you are all cooled down and feeling better! Thank you, God! Do you want to spend more time with God?' Amelia jumped up. 'Yes! A God story!'

* * *

Yvonne's eleven-year-old son, Thomas, trudged heavily into the house and threw his school bag on to the floor. When Yvonne inquired about Thomas' day, she got the usual shrug but felt in her spirit that something was worse than usual. She came into the living room and sat next to her son on the sofa. Seconds passed in silence, and then Thomas began to pour out a story of a teacher who had embarrassed and ridiculed him in front of the class for a poor choice he had made. Anger began to rise in Yvonne as she saw her son's pain and shame. They both knew that Thomas' choice had not been the best, but the consequences for him had gone beyond what was right.

Without thinking, Yvonne offered to pray with him about it. She told him that she didn't want that memory and emotion sticking to him. Surprisingly, Thomas agreed. She wrapped her arm around her son and explained that she would like to pray quickly and then give him and God space to meet about it. In a while, she would check on how things were going. Yvonne mentioned that he might want to put his hands out to show God that he was open to meet with him. Thomas nodded sullenly. 'Oh, God,' she started, 'this woman hurt and embarrassed my son and tried to stick shame on him. His heart is battered and angry and wounded. Please God, come and meet with my son. Take away all feelings and words that are holding him down, and give him your words and feelings to replace them.'

Yvonne sat next to her son as tears rolled down his face for the next five minutes, while he and God met and talked. Then his body position changed and he unfolded his arms and rested them at his side, palms up. Gradually, she sensed a peace come over Thomas and felt that it was all right to ask, 'How is it going?' Thomas nodded and said, 'Lighter. Her words weren't God's words. I'm not those things.' A weak smile spread across his face as he wiped his eyes. 'Do you want to spend more time with God?' Yvonne offered. 'Yeah, I'm gonna go and lay on my bed and think and catch and write stuff down. Call me for dinner?' Yvonne assured him that she would, and she called up after him that she'd love to hear what else God said later. With a wave, Thomas disappeared into his room, empowered to hear what God really thought of him.

An exciting side-effect

A side-effect of praying with your children is that they eventually pick up the model and begin to be confident in praying with others and with you. Don't forget to create opportunities for them to pray with you or with a sibling. It is important for them to feel purposeful and powerful as ministers as well as people who receive help. There is nothing that will make you more proud than to see your children praying with their siblings, or to have them help you connect with God. It is an awesome thing!

* ✱ *

Two men chatted quietly at the back while the children gathered in small groups to catch from God and pray for each other. It was an unusual Sunday morning: the adults had gone out into seminar groups, and the children were left to meet in their groups in the main church building. Leaders huddled on the ground with the children, encouraging and supporting them as they connected with God. Two ten-year-old boys approached me to tell me that they had finished. My eyes wandered to the two men at the back of the church, and I asked the boys to follow me as I approached them.

I gently interrupted the friendly conversation, explained that the children had been growing in prayer, and asked if the two men would like the children to pray with them. They kindly agreed, and I left the boys to it. As I watched from a distance, the men stood up and the boys began to pray with them, using the model I have described. For the next 45 minutes, the two boys stood next to the men and prayed with them, checked on them, and prayed some more. Sometimes the boys would catch something from God and felt that they should pass it on to the men. The men slowly went from standing to kneeling, to lying on the floor as they met with God, one of them crying. The boys' parents were leaders in the groups, and they fought back tears as we all watched these children connect with God and help others to connect with him as well. After the service, the parents debriefed the boys. 'How long were we praying?' the boys asked. When their parents told them, they looked amazed. 'That's crazy! It only felt like five minutes.'

* ✱ *

My husband and I were leading a 'Prayer Shack' at the back of a venue for a summer camp where we would pray with children who wanted to meet with God. We had just suffered our first miscarriage and were devastated. We had wanted to name the child Grace, and we were still just beginning to process all the emotions we were feeling. Throughout the week, we prayed with hundreds of children, all learning how to hear God's voice, and we saw God do some amazing things. One of the children who had consistently come to hear more and more from God approached us on the last day. She said that she had been catching from God, and he'd told her that he wanted her to come and pray with us.

Mark and I are always happy to be prayed with, so we knelt on the ground next to this small eight-year-old girl. She explained that she would pray for us, then we would wait and see what God wanted to do, and then she would check in on us. We had no idea what was about to happen. Evidently God had told her not only that we needed to meet with him, but also how we were feeling. With her little hands on us, she prayed, 'God, these two nice people are hurting very badly inside them, really bad, and I don't know why, but you do. They helped me a lot, and I pray that you would help them so much now. Come and meet with them loads, God.' She paused and leaned forward. 'Now we wait.' Tears poured down our faces as we met with God and he spoke to us and held us. It was the first time we had met with God as a couple about this experience. After a while, the little girl checked in: 'You OK?' We smiled and nodded as we mopped up our tears. I was worried that we might have freaked her out, but she just beamed at us. Her whole body and face were lit up. 'It's good, isn't it?' she said knowingly and skipped away. We got a brief glimpse of her name tag as she ran off. Her name was Grace.

Praying for children

I want to close with a note about praying for children rather than praying with them. This chapter has been about how to pray *with* children to facilitate their connection with God, but praying *for* your children is a wonderful thing, that you should feel free to do around them. Praying for your children is an outworking of your connection to God, and it is very beneficial for children to receive that gift from you.

My favourite childhood memories are of my dad or mum praying for me before I went to bed. I was able to hear their connection with God, along with all the intercessions and blessings that they wanted for me. I felt so loved, being connected to God and them at the same time. This process continued throughout my teenage years; even to this day, I can't get off the phone to my father before he's insisted on praying for me. I love it so much, and it gives me a glimpse of how much he must pray for me when I'm not with him or on the phone. Praying for your children is important. It models for them the way your relationship with them affects your relationship with God and vice versa. Both praying for your children and praying with your children are important to their connection with God.

*

— Chapter 8 —

Helping children who struggle to connect

Anne came to talk to me about her son, Henry. She felt at the end of her tether. No matter what she tried, she couldn't help her son connect with God. She felt as if she was doing most things right. He was growing in terms of understanding the truth of who God was, and was even chatting to God occasionally, but when it came down to hearing his voice and having conversations with God, Henry just couldn't do it. Henry was frustrated and so was she. Was this as deep a relationship as he was ever going to have with God?

What about children who struggle to connect with God? What happens if we pray and they don't catch anything? These experiences do happen and we can often feel powerless in the face of them. Sometimes, children feel as if there is a block between them and God, and, no matter what they do, it won't go away. They can feel as if there is an abrupt and disappointing ending to prayer. However, there are some tools we can use to help them find a way forward and connect with God, so, if ever our children get into these difficulties, we can be proactive in helping them get out. We need to remember that there are no dead ends for God.

We discussed in a previous chapter the importance of perseverance and of viewing our relationship with God as a journey of connection and recognition (see pages 85–86). We need to keep encouraging our children in this, but we can also take some very practical steps in helping them tackle any obstacles. I am going to use two examples of real children's experiences to illustrate those steps. The children are Nathan and Jo.

There was a child in my church, Nathan, who had a year-long

journey towards connecting with God. He was seven years old and, when we first told him about God speaking to people, he was adamant that God didn't do that. After a few months of watching children in church build a two-way relationship with God and meet with him over and over again, he began to acknowledge that maybe God did speak, but just not to him. Nathan would sit in church when children were offered one-to-one time with God, but he would just watch and refuse to try for himself. Then he began to try casually, expecting that it wouldn't work. If it didn't happen instantly, he quickly gave up, seemingly affirmed in his belief that God wouldn't speak to him. Nathan was trapped in the cycle of a mismatch between truth and experience: he had created false expectations of who God was and the way they were doomed to interact. After a year of this, he finally came to the point where he truly wanted to have a two-way relationship with the God we had been telling him about, and he wanted to know God's voice in his life. He was determined to try until he could hear what God was trying to say to him, so he came to us for help.

There was another child in my church, a ten-year-old girl named Jo. She was the epitome of disengagement whenever connecting with God came up. She would do everything possible to distract herself and others from wanting to connect with God and from entering into the experience. She had a lot of disruption in her life, and we could never really pin down what was wrong. One day, she came to me after church and asked to speak with me. She started crying and told me that she was desperate to connect with God but, whenever she tried, she heard nothing. She felt so lost and rejected that she had been too embarrassed to talk to anyone about it. She knew I'd said that God was speaking to everyone and wanting to live in relationship with all of us, and she wanted my help to work out how.

Identify the problem through guided discussion

When we feel frustrated, often we don't know how to describe that feeling to others. Children struggle especially with this difficulty. In order for us to lead the way forward for them, we need to understand more about their experience of the problem. We can help them learn to articulate why they feel so blocked in their encounter with God, and then we can use that imagery to open the discussion.

With seven-year-old Nathan, we asked him to draw the way he was feeling. We gave him a few suggestions but eventually he told us that he felt as if there was a huge wall between him and God. He didn't know how it had got there, but it was there and he didn't know how to move it.

Jo also felt as if there was a massive wall between her and God. When I asked her who built the wall, she paused for a second and then said that she was the one who'd built it. I decided to pursue this line, and asked what the wall was made of. She said she didn't know, but I encouraged her to ask God if he knew what the wall was made of. She sighed and closed her eyes. 'Fear,' she said, looking surprised. 'Fear of what?' She thought for a second. 'Fear of what he would think of me and what he would say if we really met.' I nodded. 'I can definitely see why you feel there is a wall between you!'

Ground their experience in truth

This step simply helps children to see that God is not flummoxed by their situation. It roots their experiences as part of their journey of relationship with God, instead of letting them think that they are on the outside, looking in. Depending on the age of the child and the situation, we can either simply tell them the biblical truth or take the time to look it up with them. We are not trying to do a five-point Bible study here; the purpose is simply to tie their experience to truth, to point them in the right direction.

In Nathan's case, my husband Mark told him that when we have been given a new life by choosing to be cleaned by Jesus, the Bible says that nothing can separate us from the love of God—nothing![1] Mark asked Nathan if he had ever asked Jesus to take away his sins and make him clean. Nathan affirmed that he had, several times. 'Well then, if you want to be close to God, nothing can stand in the way. Not even this wall.' Mark told him that he was going to pray with Nathan about it, and that they were going to ask God to knock down the wall, just like God knocked down the walls of Jericho.

With Jo, I felt it was important to show her from the Bible why fear was such a block, and how she could get rid of her fear so that she and God could meet. We looked up Romans 8:15–16, which says, 'God's Spirit doesn't make us slaves who are afraid of him. Instead, we become his children and call him our Father. God's Spirit makes us sure that we are his children.' We talked about how Father God loves us and treats us with love and gentleness. We chatted about what God is like as a father and what that means in relationship with him. Jo talked about how she often did feel like a slave who was afraid of God but had to do what he said, and she realised that that wasn't what God intended. She felt that she was ready to drop the wall. I showed her 1 John 4:18, which says that 'perfect love drives out fear' (NIV). I asked if I could pray with her so that she could take her wall down. We would then ask God to show her his love for her and drive any remaining fear away from their relationship.

Pray specifically with them regarding what you know

This is simply about taking the next step and connecting children to God using the model that we saw in the previous chapter.

Mark told Nathan that he was going to pray, and then there would be a time for Nathan and God to meet up. After a while, Mark would check back and see how it was going. Mark encouraged

Nathan to picture in his mind the wall that was between him and God, and see what God would do. He put his hand on Nathan's shoulder and suggested that Nathan hold out his arms as if he was ready to catch what God was going to pass to him. Nathan's eyes closed as Mark prayed, 'Father God, you said that nothing can separate us from your love. Nathan has felt that there is a big wall between you two. Please come now and knock down that wall, so that nothing will be between Nathan's heart and your heart.' Nathan and Mark waited for God. After a while, Mark checked in with him. 'So what did God do?' Nathan smiled, 'He knocked down the wall.'

Jo was eager to meet with God. I gave her a quick rundown of how it would go and suggested that she hold her hands out in front of her as if she was ready and open to receive what God had for her. I encouraged her that when it was time for her and God to meet, she could show him the wall and then break the wall down, so that they both knew it wasn't there any more. As she closed her eyes, I laid my hand on her shoulder and prayed, 'God, Jo has been living in fear of what a relationship with you would be like. She has built a wall that she doesn't want any more. Please fill her with your love that will drive away all fear, so that she can truly know what it is like to be your child.' As Jo and God met, I could sense a feeling of surprise and joy building within her. She and God talked for a while, and I knew that the problem wouldn't exist any longer. When I checked in with her, she wiped some tears off her face and said, 'Wow, we have a lot to talk about!' I laughed and agreed.

Decide on the next step

Each child's experience will be different, and you never know what may need to happen next until you get there. You may need to repeat some steps, you may need to try something different, or you may have finished. Often, helping a child may require a few weeks of going through this process, moving forward a little at a time.

Nathan felt connected to God but didn't feel that he knew how to hear his voice yet, so Mark decided to try something new with him to help.

Jo, on the other hand, felt that she needed some time with God to catch up, and headed off to chat and catch with him. Weeks later, she showed me a full journal of her encounters with God and said that her parents were talking through some of them with her and helping her continue on her path.

Another tool: asking direct questions

In some cases, children need a bit more guidance and practice in catching God's communications with them. I have found that it is often helpful to give them some direct questions that they can ask God and try to catch his answer. Catching from God is easier than we make it sometimes, so I tell them that I want them to catch the first words or pictures that pop into their minds when we ask God the question.

For this exercise, it is important not to doubt that first impression or say that it's too silly. We just need to trust that it is from God. Then we can start to ask God a series of questions—any questions we like that are based on relationship. The purpose of this is to help our children focus for small bursts of time and not try too hard. Often, they feel a block because they have assumed that catching from God is hard, and it's actually not. You can ask God myriad questions: When are you really proud of me? What do you like best about me? What makes your heart sad? What is your favourite time that you and I have spent together? What is one promise you have made us in the Bible that you want me to know? If you could play one game with me, what would it be and why? What Bible person do you think I'm like and why? The list goes on and on.

Mark tried this with Nathan. He suggested that Nathan should ask God, 'How do you feel about me?' They waited a few seconds and Mark checked in again. Nathan looked up, surprised and excited: 'He said that he was proud of me!' 'That's really cool!' Mark affirmed. 'That definitely sounds like God was talking to you. Want to ask more?' Mark led Nathan through two more questions, and his confidence in hearing God grew. Over the next couple of months, he not only learned to recognise God's voice but he also began to notice when he wasn't hearing from God and to dismiss his wayward thoughts. He became a transformed child, loving God and being loved. His parents continued to work with him at home, empowering and helping him with his chatting and catching.

Nathan became one of our prime worship leaders and a role model for the rest of the group. When we did group listening in church, and I asked who had struggled that day to hear from God, he would come right alongside those people, patting them on the back and encouraging them to keep going. One day he stood up and gave a brief speech, telling his story and saying emphatically that no one must give up but must keep trying, because it is so worthwhile every time God talks. I think that if Nathan's parents and I had been satisfied with having taught him just to know *about* God, he would have missed all the joy of God and all the experience of perseverance, leadership, testimony, connection and openness that he subsequently gained.

Keep encouraging, modelling and proactively discipling

The struggle to connect is only a part of your children's journey of relationship with God, but sometimes it can feel all-consuming. It is very important for our children that we help them to see that there is more to their relationship with God than this struggle. They are growing in their knowledge about God, in sharing their lives with him, and in seeing the truth of him in the experiences of their lives and the reality of the lives around them. Currently, this struggle is theirs to walk through, but they will come out the other side. They need to know that you and God are walking with them, encouraging them and helping them stay connected while it seems difficult.

God is always speaking, and he is faithful to help you and your children learn how to break through any difficulties in front of you. God will also speak to you about it, so, if you feel that you lack wisdom, ask him. He knows the depths of your child's heart and knows the way forward. He promises in Jeremiah 33:3, 'Call to me and I will answer you and tell you great and unsearchable things you do not know' (NIV). Sometimes we just need to call to him!

Note
1.   Romans 8:38–39

*

Part Three

Implementing a plan

*

— Chapter 9 —

Creating a plan for all ages

The parents settled slowly into their chairs, hot steamy cups of tea in their hands and weary smiles on their faces. It was Week Four of our five-week parenting course on helping children connect with God, and I could tell something was wrong. After the compulsory preliminaries, I jumped in to ask the reason for the mood. 'It just seems like so much!' Darren said, as the others nodded along. 'I have three children who are completely different in every way, including their spiritual life. There is so much to think of, so much I want to model and proactively do with them, but I can't do it all at once.'

How do we approach the proactive discipling of our children when there is so much we want to communicate to them and guide them towards? We can all feel overwhelmed by questions about how to move forward. In this chapter, we are going to create a plan. The intention is not to be rigid or formal or to create a formula for us to perform. This plan will simply help us to organise our thoughts and dreams into one place, and to be calmly in control of the way we choose to help our children grow in their relationship with God. To help order our thoughts, we will be writing them into a chart with three columns. Every child is different, so I would encourage you to make a separate chart for each of your children.

Creating a plan

First column: Vision

In order to begin writing a plan, we need to have a clear direction in mind. This goal needs to be firm in our heads and secure in our hearts. Think about playing snakes and ladders. I don't know about you, but I always tend to be slightly confused and disoriented when playing that game. I know the goal, but most of the time I have no idea which way I'm heading. I was going towards the left, but I've just shot up the board, and now I'm going right—no, left, right? Then I have to squint really hard at the squares to read the numbers so that I can get my bearings. If another player is on the same row, I have no idea who is winning until I am super-close to the goal.

If we don't clearly know the direction in which we are heading, we can easily get discouraged. If we know where we are going and the path we plan to take, then we can see our progress, celebrate it and identify easily when we have gone off course. Proactively discipling our children requires us to have a direction and a plan.

Each one of us has a long-term vision of our desires for our children spiritually. It fuels us, frustrates us and drives us to want to do better, to help them get there. Our long-term vision and dreams make today's efforts worthwhile because we want to see something wonderful in their lives tomorrow. Creating a plan will help us to be strategic and deliberate in aiming our spiritual influence towards that goal.

On the far left column of our chart, we will be writing our answer to the question, 'In ten years' time, what do I want my child's relationship with God to look like?' It is helpful to break this question down into specific aspects of each of your children's relationships with God. For example, if I had a two-year-old and a seven-year-old, the beginnings of my charts may look like this.

Ezekiel: two years old

In ten years, I want him to...		
Love being in God's presence.		
Own his relationship with God.		
Know how to access God through the Bible.		
Be confident in hearing God's voice.		
Make brave choices that honour God.		

Tabitha: seven years old

In ten years, I want her to...		
Proactively seek time with God on her own.		
Know her gifts and purpose and serve others with them.		
Explore the Bible for answers and meet with God through it.		
Hear God's voice consistently and accurately.		

Be solid in her identity and the self-image God has given to her, and renew her identity with him on an ongoing basis.		
Run to God when she is sad or ashamed.		

This would be only the very beginning of my vision column, and I would encourage you to create a nice long list of the specific dreams you have for your children. The more detailed they are, the better you will be able to see clear ways forward. Take some time to think through all the sections of this book and your own experiences of faith to fill out a healthy, balanced vision for each of your children.

Second column: Spiritually, where is my child now?

Now that we know the goals we are working towards, we need to know the starting point. It is crucial that we understand where our children are on the journey, so that we know how best to move them forward.

Looking at your charts, take some time to fill in specific and honest responses to the question of where your children are on their journeys in terms of your ten-year vision. Don't try to make the situation better or worse than it is. This is just the starting place. This exercise isn't intended to show how big the gaps are, but to empower us to make wise and accurate decisions on the way forward. The more honest we are, the better we position ourselves to act.

Many of us may not know the answers to some of the points. If that is the case, I would encourage you to try to find out. You don't have to pin your eleven-year-old to the wall and force out a progress report or try to get your three-year-old to verbalise her current view of prayer. You are their parent or prime carer: you know them well. Put your antennae up, ask questions, check out their reactions and pray about them. Once you have a good feel, you will be able to fill in the chart with confidence. You may not be able to work out some aspects yet. Don't worry: just leave them blank. Over the next months and years, you will eventually be able to pinpoint the child's starting points in different areas, and you can then begin to be more proactive as necessary.

My abbreviated chart may now look like this:

Ezekiel: two years old

In ten years, I want him to...	Currently, he...	
Love being in God's presence.	Is aware of himself as a person and is growing in his understanding of relationship.	
Own his relationship with God.	Is responding to God when I pray with him and for him, but isn't aware of what a personal relationship would be.	
Know how to access God through the Bible.	Can't read.	
Be confident in hearing God's voice.	Can't identify God's voice.	
Make brave choices that honour God.	Is learning independence and the power of his choices; is learning about consequences.	

Tabitha: seven years old

In ten years, I want her to...	Currently, she...	
Proactively seek time with God on her own.	Is OK spending time with me while I am spending time with God, but doesn't really engage.	
Know her gifts and purpose and serve others with them.	Likes helping with things, but doesn't feel particularly gifted by God with anything.	
Explore the Bible for answers and meet with God through it.	Likes looking through picture story books of the Bible, but hates reading the Bible.	
Hear God's voice consistently and accurately.	Has heard God a couple of times, but isn't confident in those experiences. Sometimes doubts that God exists; other times totally convinced and seeking.	
Be solid in her identity and the self-image God has given to her, and renew her identity with him on an ongoing basis.	Chases after the latest fad and scares me with how much she takes on board from TV and movies.	
Run to God when she is sad or ashamed.	Hides and cries, and resists praying.	

This gives us a good view of the starting points, and may have helped us to look at aspects of our children's spiritual lives that we have never considered before. We are now well grounded to answer the next question.

Third column: What is the next step for my child, and how can I help him or her take it?

The third column is what we live for—moving our children closer and closer to God and a life with him, with practical, achievable, fruit-producing steps. This column will not be a list of 101 things that we are going to do right now. It is just an aid to thinking through the next step for your children in each area and what you could do to help them take that next step. There are no right answers here, as the next steps are inextricably linked with who your children are and what their lives look like. The next step for one child may be very different for another in exactly the same situation.

For example, my sample charts would look like this:

Ezekiel: two years old

In ten years, I want him to...	Currently, he...	The next step for him is...
Love being in God's presence.	Is aware of himself as a person and is growing in his understanding of relationship.	To be able to recognise God's presence. I can help by creating situations at home, at church and in town where he can be in God's presence, and I will verbally help him recognise consistently what that is like.

Own his relationship with God.	Is responding to God when I pray with him and for him, but isn't aware of what a personal relationship would be.	To understand that people can have a relationship with God. I can help by telling him Bible stories and life stories of what life is like in relationship with God, and point out similarities between the stories and his circumstances so that he can begin to see God's influence in his life.
Know how to access God through the Bible.	Can't read.	To see how important the Bible is. I can help by making sure I refer to the Bible in front of him, to show how helpful it is to me.
Be confident in hearing God's voice.	Can't identify God's voice.	To know about the different ways we can catch from God and have the opportunity to do so. I can help by telling stories and making pictures on the wall of how God talks to us, and by modelling when he speaks to me. I can also make sure, at bedtime prayers, that I invite God to speak and give him space to do so.
Make brave choices that honour God.	Is learning independence and the power of his choices; is learning about consequences.	To grow in making choices well. I can help by creating opportunities to make brave and wise choices, identifying them and affirming him when he makes those choices.

Tabitha: seven years old

In ten years, I want her to...	Currently, she...	The next step for her is...
Proactively seek time with God on her own.	Is OK spending time with me while I am spending time with God, but doesn't really engage.	To know what is on offer for her. I can help by being more verbal in my modelling of my encounters with God, so that she knows the benefits of this time in my life. I can also invite her more explicitly into encountering God by explaining how to chat to God and catch from him.
Know her gifts and purpose and serve others with them.	Likes helping with things, but doesn't feel particularly gifted by God with anything.	To connect with God so that she can hear from him all the treasure he has put inside her and the gifts he has given her. I can help by affirming what I see in her, comparing her with people in the Bible who had the same gifts, and continuing to teach her how to connect with God's voice.
Explore the Bible for answers and meet with God through it.	Likes looking through picture story books of the Bible, but hates reading the Bible.	To know how to access the Bible. I can help by getting her a topical concordance and helping her learn how to search the Bible for herself without having to read it cover to cover. I can also get her some topical reading notes that would help her apply the Bible to her relationship with God.

Hear God's voice consistently and accurately.	Has heard God a couple of times, but isn't confident in those experiences. Sometimes doubts that God exists; other times totally convinced and seeking.	To discard some views of God that are getting in the way. I can help by being more proactive in conversations with her about it, and I can make some observations about how she responds to God. I can also offer to pray with her to help her get over any blocks she is feeling, and I can help bring some biblical truth to her erratic experiences with God.
Be solid in her identity and the self-image God has given to her, and renew her identity with him on an ongoing basis.	Chases after the latest fad and scares me with how much she takes onboard from TV and movies.	To begin to chat with God about how she feels. I think a big part of her behaviour is her way of coping with peer pressure. I can help by modelling how to chat to God in my life and encouraging her to chat on her own.
Run to God when she is sad or ashamed.	Hides and cries, and resists praying.	To stop hiding from vulnerability with God. I can help by modelling that it is OK and helpful to do that. Right now, I am modelling that I'm always OK and that I should just swallow what I feel. I need to model by small debriefs, in an appropriate and non-scary way, how helpful running to God is.

Some of these next steps might overlap. If so, fantastic! You can be super-efficient. Sometimes, just one or two 'next steps' can mean seeing progress in your child across many different sections of your vision chart.

Implementing the plan

Pace yourself

Now that you have your chart, you need to decide how to implement it. There is no one way to do this. It is completely up to you and the way your family works. Every child is different and will be able to move at a different pace, so don't feel that you must address every section at the same time. Spend some time with God and with any other adults who are in partnership with you, helping you parent your child towards these goals. Decide on the goals that you feel are most important now, and those that you feel you can do well now. Some will be easy fixes and some may take a while, but as long as you are being proactive and ensuring that you are modelling your faith, you are on the right path. These are long-term goals, and you can have a long-term strategy.

Celebrate and modify as you go

The charts will be constantly modified as you move along the journey. As your children get older, all three columns will need adjustment. You might add some new aspects of the vision, update your children's current spiritual position, and adjust and set new next steps. Sometimes children are ripe for growth in one area, and you see great movement; other areas may take longer. Find a good balance between sticking with your plan and celebrating what God is doing in their lives at the moment.

Building next steps by tying together truth and relational experience

Remember that, as we implement the next steps, we need to keep tying together truth and relational experience. It is easy to grow just one or the other, but the most efficient way is to grow them together. We may have had to do some work with our children to fix the separation and, as we move forward, it is essential that we do not allow it to occur again. There are many simple ways of doing this.

Testimony

Invite others into family times to share about what God has been doing in their lives. Ask questions that lead them to talk about how biblical truth and their experience of a living relationship with God work together.

Answering questions

Often, when our children ask questions, we can answer quite specifically. This is an opportunity to ensure that our answer includes both biblical truth and relational experience, so that our children can process these aspects as a whole instead of having to make assumptions about one or the other. I was once asked by a six-year-old, 'Does Jesus love people in hell?' The answer to that question can vary depending on the age of the child. One answer for the six-year-old, tying together truth and experience, is, 'Yes he does. It says in the Bible that God loves everyone and wants everyone to live with him.[1] Jesus is really sad when people choose to live their eternal lives apart from him, because he came to save everybody from being lost and in the dark.'

With slightly older children, you may want to open the Bible and look up the verses together to help them understand what the Bible says, and then encourage them to ask God how he feels about people in hell and catch his answer. I know one child who has a question-and-answer book, and she writes her questions down, catches the answer from God, and then looks up verses in the Bible to round out and ground the answer. An added benefit to this is that, if the question arises again, she can look it up and show her friends.

Sometimes children just need a quick answer, and sometimes they are willing and interested enough to sit with you and look in the Bible. Only you will know what is right in the moment. If you have been doing this with them throughout their childhood, you may be able to empower them more and more to find the answer for themselves. By the time I was a teenager, my mother would expect me to have done some connecting with God and some biblical research before I came to her with a question. If I hadn't, she would tell me that she'd love to chat about it with me and help me think it through when I had done so.

Empowering biblical access

Just as we have looked at empowering our children to connect with God's heart through hearing and recognising his voice and chatting to him, we also need to ensure that we are empowering them to access his voice and wisdom through the Bible. This is not just about helping them connect with God through his words, but also about teaching them how to use the Bible as a tool to light their path. It is important to give them this knowledge-based tool so that when their experiences with life and with God raise the need, they are fully able to reach into his word and find what they need to bolster their relationship with him.

- Help them to memorise the books of the Bible: If children know where to find each book, it turns the Bible from a huge, confusing book to a book that they know their way around. There are many songs that will help them memorise the books of the Bible. My mum put them to a tune I already knew, and by the age of four it was firmly in my head. This is still the way I find places in the Bible today. (Try it for yourself. The Old Testament goes to the tune of 'Jingle bells', starting with the verse rather than the chorus, and the New Testament is to the the tune of 'Twinkle, twinkle, little star'.) Why not make up your own song?

- Teach them how to look up verses in the Bible: Buy a concordance and topical concordance and model how to use them for a couple of years. Give children their own concordance once you see them using it for themselves.
- Get them a Bible with study notes and cross-referencing: If children struggle with reading, buy them the Bible on CD so that they can still feed themselves with scripture.

Remember your call

Remember, we are called to parent well, but our children have choices as they grow. Our job is to ask ourselves what is the next step for them and.help them take it, not force them to take it. We are called to equip, encourage, set boundaries and guide our children in their relationship with God, but to do it wisely, without exasperating or controlling them. God is partnering with us and is faithfully speaking to them and knocking on their heart's door.

Note
1.   John 3:16; Matthew 23:37

*

— Chapter 10 —

Starting well with under-fives

Elliott's four-year-old face scrunched up at me. 'Are dinosaurs from God?' 'Phew, an easy one for once,' I thought. 'Well, it says in the Bible that God created all things, and I see every day that he is still making new and wonderful things, so I would say, yes! Dinosaurs are from God.' Elliott's face broke out in a smile. 'I'm glad!' There is nothing on this planet that Elliott loves more than dinosaurs, and he seems to be educated to university level in all their names and details. 'This might be fun,' I thought as an idea popped into my head. 'Hey, Elliott, people make up songs to God all the time to tell him how they feel. King David did it and we can, too! Let's sing a song to God to tell him how wonderful he is for making dinosaurs.' Elliott giggled and agreed. For ten minutes we danced and sang and made up a song for God, as Elliott and I shared with God how much we loved him for being so creative. It wasn't the prettiest song in the world but it was heartfelt and fun, and we both felt God's presence as we laughed and sang.

Parents of children under five years old have a wonderful chance to build from the beginning. I am aware that some of the ideas in this book will look slightly different if you are working with under-fives, so I want to provide some practical suggestions and true stories to encourage you as you begin to implement your plan.

The first thing to say is that modelling is vital. Children are like sponges, assimilating new information at an astonishing rate. They mimic the way we talk, eat, drink, process emotions and handle social situations. Everything we do serves, for them, as a blueprint for the way the world works and how to interact with it. Modelling the reality of a relationship with God is a powerful tool for those of us with young children. We can communicate so much to them merely by being ourselves and creating windows, verbalising and inviting them in to share our experiences with God. We cannot underestimate the power our modelling carries with our children at this age. Take advantage of it!

From birth to age two

Children at this age are just beginning to make sense of the world and their place in it. So what can we do proactively to equip them and encourage them into a relationship with God?

Building a godly 'normality'

Children of this age are absorbing the way everything works and are beginning to establish a 'normal' state of life. This is a productive time to establish for them a life filled with the presence of God, prayer, worship songs and Bible stories and verses. We have the opportunity to build into the fabric of their understanding a world with God at the centre.

Connecting with God

At one church that I worked with, our ministry with babies and toddlers had the strapline 'An encounter with God is life-changing, no matter what our age'. John the Baptist leapt in his mother's womb when Elizabeth was filled with the Holy Spirit on meeting the pregnant Mary.[1] If children in the womb can perceive the presence of God, then no one is too young. There are many things we can do to help connect our children to God.

Pray for them

Even while you are pregnant, take the time to pray for your child, blessing him or her and asking for the Lord's presence. I often prayed that my baby would know the touch of the Lord more than my own, so that there was never a moment of his life when he didn't recognise God. Our children need our prayers throughout their lives, so let's start at the very beginning.

Model chatting with God for them

They may not totally understand at first, but, when they do, chatting with God will be as normal as talking to other people. They will see reality in your actions before they fully understand it. As they develop verbally, you can help them to chat with God by encouraging them at the level at which they are engaging in other relationships. I knew a mum who wanted to get her child used to the idea that God is always with us, so she began to acknowledge his real presence in the house as normal. Every once in a while, she would say, 'Why don't you show me and God your dance?' or 'Oooo, should we show God your owie? Look, God, Jenny has an owie' (that is, a scratch or any kind of wound or bruise).

Catch for them

We do a lot of things for our children when they are young, and you can start 'catching' for them right away. I know several parents who started a book for their children as soon as they were born, and, as they prayed for them, they would include in the book words or pictures that God gave them regarding the child. I met one of their children when he was four; he very proudly told me how important he was to God and how God talked to his parents about him, and now God talks to him, too. He sat with me and showed me page after page of pictures and words, and explained each one to me. It was so powerful to see a book of God's communication with this child through so many people. I was so excited to see his own drawings placed towards the end of the book, and to recognise his catching from God as a continuation of the communication God had been sending his way since before birth.

Pray with them

Although our babies and toddlers may not be able to comprehend fully what is happening, we can still pray with them and invite God to connect with our children. I have been constantly surprised by the awareness of God that tiny people can have when being prayed for. I once visited some friends who had a two-month-old baby. She was sleeping and, as I prayed silently and invited God to meet with her in her sleep, she began to smile and wiggle around. I also once prayed for a mother and child who both had thrush infections in their mouths. As I prayed, I watched the baby stop crying and become very quiet and peaceful. The baby then began to poke her mouth, squeezing her tongue. When we finished praying, the woman told me that she felt an overwhelming sense of peace, and immediately she began to feel her tongue grow warm and tingly. She felt that God was touching her and healing her, and I knew that the baby had had the very same experience with God. I don't think we will ever truly know what a baby's experience with God is, but we can definitely create opportunities for God and our children to meet, and trust him to reveal himself with care and gentleness.

Ages three to four

Children of this age are growing in independence and self-expression. This age requires a lot of modelling and proactive inclusion. As they grow in independence, we can ensure that our inclusion times are individually empowering as well as corporate. These can be useful times of empowering them to build a relationship with God.

Building a right view of God

Children of this age are gathering information to piece together a view of individual people, situations and life in general. We can partner them in this search for building blocks by ensuring that we provide a wide range of biblical truth linked to relational experience, which they can use to create a right view of God.

- Give your child a wide range of Bible stories and, in the creative telling of the story, share what God was doing and thinking during the story.
- Encourage your child to read the stories to you, and ask questions about the relationship between the characters and God.
- Help frame life experiences by referring back to the Bible, so that your child can begin to see how you use scripture to think through issues and root yourself when life is confusing. You might say, 'Whew, I'm feeling very tired and wobbly. I wonder what God says in the Bible about what I should do?' Pick up the Bible and look up Matthew 11:28: 'God says, "If you are tired from carrying heavy burdens, come to me and I will give you rest." That sounds great! How can I go to God? Let's lie on the floor and ask God to give me rest!' You can also pick one or two Bible verses that are particularly applicable to your family's life circumstances and refer to them throughout the day!
- Be prepared to unwind wrong views of God. The very way in which our children's brains are maturing means that they will inevitably link things together that were not meant to go together. Keep an eye out for any mistaken view of God that pops up, so that you can correct it quickly. As we saw earlier, we ourselves can contribute to these wrong views, as we are not perfect. It is no problem; we just need to be aware so that we can fix it. Once, I was teaching three- to four-year-olds at church and we were talking about the stories of Jesus raising people from the dead. Unfortunately, I wasn't paying close attention to the words

I was using as I explained that Jesus talked to the dead people and they got up and walked around again, and ate and drank. The children's reaction wasn't what I expected. After some play and craft time, a fellow leader took me aside and suggested that I redescribe the story, as many of the children were freaked out because they were under the impression that Jesus went around making zombies.

• Be aware of the difference between 'real' and 'pretend'. Children of this age are just learning about that difference, and it is helpful to be very clear with our children that God is real and so is our relationship with him. It is worth thinking through our choices when we look at myths like Father Christmas, the Tooth Fairy and the Easter Bunny, as our children trust us to help them define 'real' and 'pretend'. Let's look at the example of Father Christmas: he sees all our deeds, lives far away, has magical powers and visits us. Belief in him is essential to make the whole relationship work. Some children are encouraged to communicate with him and believe in the evidence of his visits that are left behind—that is, presents. Some children even get to meet him and have conversations with him in his grotto. He loves all the children of the world and can seemingly be everywhere at once in one night. When we insist to our children that Father Christmas is real and encourage a belief in and relationship with him—and then do the same regarding God— we can be preparing our children for a huge faith wobble when they eventually realise that we were leading them astray about Father Christmas. Many children wonder if we were doing the same about God. It is worth thinking through how you would like to handle that moment, or, if you have yet to choose what to say about Father Christmas, it is worth considering how best to proceed.[2]

Connecting with God

By this age, children are beginning to recognise God's voice and are learning how to respond. It can be an exciting time for us as we can begin to see a two-way relationship between our child and God emerging.

Chatting to God

Children at this age are becoming very verbal. If you are modelling chatting to God and are proactively creating times for them to do this themselves, it can begin to grow into a habit. Many parents report that they hear their children chatting away to God while playing alone in their rooms, or in the dark while they are in bed, waiting to drift off to sleep.

Catching from God

Children of this age can begin to get a handle on how to catch from God, but will make a lot of mistakes. Train yourself to watch carefully, affirm their efforts and help them to discern. This is a very vulnerable time, as children can be easily squashed by us in their efforts. God is faithful to speak, I promise, and you will be surprised at what happens. Here are a few experiences that parents have shared with me:

Susie and her two children were travelling in the car when the three-year-old child, Rose, started insisting that her one-year-old brother Daniel should sleep in their mother's room that night, because of the bangs and booms that God had told her were coming. Rose's mum made some positive noises but dismissed the idea in her head. Daniel had not been sleeping well, and everyone had been getting more and more exhausted. Later that night, she thought about it again and decided that she would listen to what her daughter had heard from God, so moved her son into her own room for the night. In the middle of the night, a loud unforecasted thunderstorm struck. Daniel stirred, but quickly Susie put her hand on his back. Comforted, he dropped right back off to sleep. Susie's husband reported the next day that, although the thunderstorm had kept him awake, both Susie and Daniel had had the best night of sleep they'd experienced in three weeks.

Jack was walking down the road with his mum, Lesley, when all of a sudden he stopped abruptly and said, 'I think God just talked to me! I felt it in my tummy!' (Lesley had not yet told him about all the ways he could catch from God, just that God spoke to people.) 'What did he say?' She asked excitedly. 'Be good,' Jack replied with his eyes glowing. Lesley was baffled. 'How do you know it was God? What did it feel like?' Jack thought for a second: 'Funny.' 'Funny exciting or funny scary?' Jack sighed and rolled his eyes. 'Both, because it was God!' Lesley told him the story of how Samuel in the Bible heard God for the first time. Jack nodded knowingly, fully identifying with Samuel's experience.

I received a phone call from our close friend Mikel at around 8.00pm. He has two small children and evidently my name had come up in his nightly prayers with his three-year-old daughter. 'Um, this may sound weird, but I just wanted to check! Elizabeth was praying tonight, and she prayed specifically for your leg to get better. Is there anything wrong with it?' My jaw dropped and I explained that, earlier in the day, I had severely twisted my leg and it was massively swollen. Mikel laughed a little bit and said, 'Well, you should know then that God told Elizabeth, and she was praying for you!'

Praying with our children

With this age group, we can easily modify the model of praying with our children described in Chapter 7. It is just a matter of explaining a bit more and shrinking your waiting time to between ten and 30 seconds. You can also begin to invite your children to pray with you in the same way.

Worship is another great way for this age group to connect with God. Be aware that there are two types of songs available: truth songs that talk about God and who he is and what he is like (for example, 'Our God is a great big God'), and worship songs that help us communicate our feelings to God and help to create space for him to meet with us (for example, 'I love you, Lord'). Both can be helpful, but in different ways. Truth songs are great for imparting biblical foundations of truth in which to root our lives. Worship songs are useful for helping children to learn to connect with God by expressing their feelings for him, and encouraging them to expect to meet him. I would suggest using both types.

Working with children's development stages

Remember, we are working on a real relationship with a real God. It is helpful, therefore, to look at how your children are relating to other children and family members: this will be a good guide to help you understand what your child is ready for and how to help.

- Look at the way you are guiding them in their relationships. How are you helping them express themselves? What do they like to do with their friends? How do you empower those relationships?
- Consider the level of their independence. How confident are they in talking to other children or adults?
- What is the emotional depth of their relationships? What do they talk about with you? What do they chat about with their friends?

We can expect the same level of interaction with God. We some-times mistakenly expect a more mature level of relationship with God than is normal in our children's ordinary relational lives. Don't be surprised if their entire 'chat' time with God is about butterflies or Dora the Explorer. Sharing the little things opens the door for them to share bigger things. As in their everyday relationships, they might need some prompting to talk about their feelings with God. If you feel that that is the next step, encourage and guide them into doing it.

Every child is different and will progress at different levels at different times. Just as some children of the same age are adept at gross motor skills and some at fine motor skills, our children may be at different levels spiritually from those around them. What matters is that they eventually emerge balanced, so encourage what is going well and gently nudge them in places of growth. As you help your children to take their next step towards God, he is faithful to meet with them at each unique stage and connect with them right where they are.

Notes

1. Luke 1:41
2. If you choose to not 'do' Father Christmas with your children, it is helpful to know that they may have to cope with some peer issues at playgroup or school. This is a prime time for preparing your child with a framework before they have to face the actual situation. You could take some time talking about how much fun the 'Father Christmas' game is to many people. It is helpful to discuss with them that it isn't our job to ruin the game for others. If you participate in community events with Father Christmas or Santa's Grotto, you and your child could agree that it would be OK to play the pretend game at times, while making sure they themselves know that it is still 'pretend'. You could do some play scenarios of what to say if other children ask questions of your child. You could talk about peer pressure in the Bible and how people in the Bible coped with it. There are many times in our culture when we will have to do something similar, Halloween included. This is just the first of many occasions when you will have to coach your child through life in a world of conflicted values and beliefs.

*

— Chapter 11 —

FAQs

Are 'thank you', 'sorry' and 'please' still good things to pray?

In any relationship, these things are important to say! The key is that they need to be embedded in a relationship, instead of working as the basis for one. As your children grow closer to God, these words will begin to appear naturally in their prayers. I would suggest that you take a lead in modelling the heart-connected way of expressing your thanks, your feelings about sins and your requests through chatting informally. It may be helpful to use only one of these in the midst of a wider chat about life, so that your children can see it as a part of communication with God, but not the only part.

My child is a very kinaesthetic learner. What about creative prayer?

I have found that people often use creative prayer as a desperate way of making prayer and God 'fun'. The problem is that it can encourage children to make a connection to the activity and not to God. I would suggest working on heart-to-heart connection with God through chatting and catching first. I'm sure you can find creative, active ways of showing children how to chat and catch, but it is important that they know how to access God personally. Your child can connect with you through listening to you and chatting to you, and he or she will be able to do the same with God. Too often, we try to insert an 'activity' to help our children, but the activity ends up getting in the way.

This doesn't mean that chat and catch need to be done while sitting down in the quiet. I know children who go on bike rides to chat with God and hear his voice. Other children perform 'chat dances' for God to show him how they feel, and some listen to music to hear his voice. Some prefer to sculpt the pictures God gives them instead of writing them down. These ideas have come out of the children's desire to spend time with God, and they have decided on their own initiative to use these methods.

Once the relationship is established, there are many ways to enhance it by adding creativity to the two-way communication. I would suggest, though, that the connection is established first, so that creativity is a natural individual development instead of *the* way of praying.

I have a daughter who is very anti-God, encouraged by my unbelieving partner. What do I do?

Many families are in your same situation, and it is never easy. My main suggestion is to model the reality of your relationship with God and to create and implement your plan. Your child needs to see that God is real and is powerful in your life, and that she can have the same relationship with him that you have. You can pray for her and invite her to tell you things that she would especially like you to bring to God. She may brush you aside but at least she knows that you are consistently bringing her to the real God, whom you know personally. It may be hard to see an immediate way forward, but these are long-term goals.

Perhaps a further step would be to look at her experience with God and see if she has formed some wrong views of God that need to be unwound. Many children who are anti-God are rooted in a particular (incorrect) belief about who he is, and are rejecting that belief. Most children I know don't want to be controlled or forced, but, if you are just modelling and asking questions about her views, there is very little for her to object to. Also remember that God is longing to connect with her. He is speaking to her and is faithful to wait for her response, so you have a partner in your desires.

What about our family times when we study the Bible and pray together? Are all corporate experiences bad?

Family times are brilliant! This is an expression of what God wanted for all believers—to live and encourage each other in community and praise him together. Family times can be especially powerful when you chat to God together about life and catch from him what he wants to say to your family as a whole. Discussion and learning in the home are part of the way God designed us to learn to love him. It is all about balance: both corporate and individual times create a healthy, growing relationship with God.

What do I do when my child becomes a teenager?

Keep implementing your plan! Your approach may begin to need some adjustment, as will all your parenting, as you allow your child to be more independent and to make mistakes. You will then become more of a mentor, ready to help, equip and challenge when and where it is appropriate.

Remember that children will be in a different emotional state when they are teenagers, so you can begin to expand the complexity of what you are trying to develop in them. They will be able to see the Bible and their relationship with God differently, and they will have a more mature view of both. Take some time to go back over the Bible stories that they knew in their childhood and show them new insights about them. The stories of Noah and the flood[1] and Peter's denial of Jesus[2] are really helpful studies in peer pressure. It is important that we train our children to draw new and relevant truth out of well-known stories. Teenagers are also ready to understand more about how their life choices reflect their relationship with God. They are ready to begin learning from the Bible about wisdom and character, holiness and struggle, persecution and faithfulness in their walk with him.

I have grown-up children, and I feel bad that I didn't do this with them when they were children. Is it too late?

I firmly believe that it is never too late. Your children know you and watch you, so you still have plenty of opportunities to model the reality of your relationship with God in front of them.

Chatting to God out loud? My child will think I've gone crazy! I don't think I could do that. Won't it look weird or fake?

I don't deny that it may feel a bit strange to you at first, but how else are your children going to know what is going on in your head between you and God? You know how best to introduce this practice into your family. Maybe, with yours, it will need a gradual build-up. I agree that going from nothing to chatting out loud 15 times a day may be a bit of a shock, but if you gradually build up over three months, your children will barely notice. Many people I've worked with wondered about this at the beginning of their journey, but all are glad that they did it.

I'm not very confident in 'catching' from God myself. Will I be able to help my child?

Yes, you will. We are all on individual journeys with God, and perhaps God wants you to work with him on this aspect of your relationship with him now. There is a great book called *Can You Hear Me?* by Brad Jersak,[3] which is very helpful for adults who want to grow in their ability to hear God. I would suggest that you read it; then, as you grow, you can help your children grow.

My child isn't a very good reader, and all this 'discernment and truth-reinforcing' sounds as if it needs a lot of Bible reading. How can I help my child access the Bible when he hates reading?

Many children struggle with reading, and often it seems impossible that they would ever enjoy reading the Bible. I think we need to expand our ideas of how to empower our children to access the Bible. Many of us feel that the main access route is to read our Bibles consistently every day. For children who struggle, this may not be an option. There are plenty of Bibles on CD, and you can partner your child in developing a way to remember the things she has heard. One family I know has a box of index cards on the table, so if anyone reads or hears anything from the Bible that they like, they can write it down and save it for the family. In order to write down a verse in this way, a child may have to listen to it on the CD a couple of times, which gets it even more strongly into their heads. The cards can then be used whenever the family wants to refer to something.

The goal is for your children to learn how to access the Bible when they want the answer to a question, encouragement or a confirmation of God's promises. This doesn't require vast amounts of reading; it just requires that you equip them to find the information they need quickly. Concordances are exceedingly helpful. There is a variety of types, including alphabetical (where you look up the word you want), topical, and everything in between. Take your children to a bookshop and find what is right for them.

When is it right for my child to become a Christian? What am I supposed to do to help it happen? How do I explain it?

There is no right answer to this question, as children will be ready when they are ready. Our job is to surround them with the truth and teach them how to access God and his new life for them when they are ready. In the normal course of your parenting, you will be teaching them about sin and what Jesus did for us on the cross. You can tell your testimony and help them understand what it means for their lives and their relationship with God that Jesus has provided a way for us to get clean.

Children love stories, and one way I explain about becoming a Christian is to use the story of the father and the sandbox (see Chapter 4, pp. 55–56). It is important that we teach our children how to ask to be taken out of the sand and be given a new clean life with God. You can tell your children that if they want help in asking God to give them a new clean life, you would love to do so at any time. After that, you can just be available when your children decide that it is important to them. Instead of leading them in a prayer, you can facilitate their own communication with God, helping them to express their feelings about their sin and current life and what they want from God. You may be surprised at what emerges. Remember, becoming a Christian isn't about praying a prayer. It's about responding to what Jesus did and to the call of God on our hearts, and wanting to change the way we live in relationship with him. We are all constantly in a process of responding to the gospel and committing and recommitting ourselves to the journey, and this is an exciting first step.

How do I get my child to engage with church? He is so bored at the moment, and I don't know what to do.

We can involve our churches in our spiritual parenting, no matter what church we attend, whether it has a massive children's ministry or no children's work at all. We are training our children to know how to connect their hearts to God's heart in every circumstance, including church. Many of the concepts covered in this book apply to the church setting. In my experience of working in churches, there are two prime factors that inform how a child connects with God in a service. The first is that those responsible for that child model participation, and the second is that they proactively disciple the child by setting boundaries and expectations on his or her participation.

Modelling will be very important in showing your child how to engage with a church service. I know it can be hard, but sometimes we are so busy wrangling with our children that we don't show them how we connect with God in the service itself. Children need to see their parents worshipping, listening to the sermon, reading the Bible and responding to the message. They need to hear their parents verbalising about how meeting with God during the service helped them, and they need to be invited into the experience.

The other factor is the proactive setting of boundaries for our children at church. This is a hot topic, I know, and we all have our own opinion. I have seen many churches in action, and I am constantly amazed by the number of children completely disengaged from the service at the back of the building. Some are running around, chatting to friends, playing games or lying on the floor, reading or colouring. Others sit in the pews or chairs, wrapped in their own worlds of iPods, books or video games. While I understand that parts of the service may be boring to them, allowing our children to completely disengage and 'survive' the service doesn't help them connect with God at all.

The children I see who are really engaged with church tend to have a basic set of boundaries in place: they sit in the pews or chairs next to the person responsible for them and engage with the worship and prayer right from the beginning of the service. If there are points when children will be unable to engage, they can be challenged about their relationship with God in some other age-appropriate way (such as reading a book or the Bible, writing in a journal and so on).

When a child is under the age of four, the boundaries may be quite loose: you might hold your child and bounce her during worship, provide crayons so that she can colour on the notice sheet during the announcements, and create some space next to you so that she can play with some Noah's ark toys during the sermon (if there are no children's groups available). Children aged nine and over may participate in everything, but during the sermon they may want also to read or write while they casually listen. You may expect your teenager to participate in everything. If you have been helping your children to learn how to connect with God at home, they will already know how to do it. It is just a matter of creating the right circumstances so that they can learn how to engage while at church and how to benefit from the experience.

Notes
1. Genesis 6—7
2. Matthew 26:69–75; Mark 14:66–72; Luke 22:54–62; John 18:15–18, 25–27
3. Brad Jersak, *Can You Hear Me?* (Fresh Wind Press, 2006)

Bible index

Old Testament

New Testament

Also by Rachel Turner

Parenting Children for a Life of Purpose

Empowering children to become who they are called to be

'Too long we have stood apart as a church and looked at children and teens and said, "We love you, we value you, but we don't need you."'

Our churches have the power to establish a community of purpose that all people participate in. We can be the place where children feel most powerful, most seen, most discipled and most released. We can be the church that God designed. *Parenting Children for a Life of Purpose* is a practical and tested handbook exploring the possibilities for helping children to discover their specific gifts for what God is calling them to be, and how parents might partner with churches to enable children to discover their true identity and purpose in life and walk alongside them on the journey.

Addressing issues of identity, relationship, purpose, power, love, calling and response, each chapter includes true stories and questions to help us to reflect on our own experiences.

ISBN 978 0 85746 163 6   £7.99
Available from your local Christian bookshop or direct from BRF: visit www.brfonline.org.uk.

Also available on Kindle: see www.brfonline.org.uk/ebooks.

Parenting Children for a Life of Confidence by Rachel Turner will be available from October 2015.

Also from BRF

Creative Ways to tell a Bible Story

Techniques and tools for exploring the Bible with children and families

Martyn Payne

Creative Ways to tell a Bible Story contains a wealth of tried-and-tested ideas designed to lift any Bible story off the page and into the hearts and minds of children and adults.

The resource offers a treasure trove of ideas for opening up a Bible story (the way in), telling the story (the way through) and exploring the meaning of the story (the way out), including suggestions for reflecting on how to apply the story to our lives today.

In addition, there is a selection of over 30 key words or phrases offering ways in which connecting threads might be explored, a suggested year's programme using the Bible stories explored in the book, and a chronological index of all the Bible stories mentioned designed to enable users to find material for a particular children's session, special event, workshop or all-age church service.

ISBN 978 0 85746 113 1   £8.99
Available from your local Christian bookshop or direct from BRF: visit www.brfonline.org.uk.

Exploring God's Love in Everyday Life

Readings to help children grow in their faith

Yvonne Morris

A reflective, interactive resource for children's and family workers, parents, carers and grandparents

How do we understand Christ's love better?

Taking 1 Corinthians 13 as its starting point, *Exploring God's Love in Everyday Life* uses readings, reflections and prayers to explore the love that Jesus lived and taught. The material covers 20 themes and touches on 40 different Bible stories, seeking to nurture adults and children alike in engaging with issues of faith and life.

Based on wording from Ephesians 3:18, each section is structured as follows:

- Wide: A key story that presents the general concept of the theme
- Long: A second story that offers a different angle on the theme
- High: Wondering and chatting together about this aspect of love
- Deep: Connecting with God through prayer and listening

ISBN 978 0 85746 021 9   £6.99
Available from your local Christian bookshop or direct from BRF: visit www.brfonline.org.uk.

Enjoyed

![brf logo]

this book?

Write a review—we'd love to hear what you think.
Email: reviews@brf.org.uk

Keep up to date—receive details of our new books as they happen.
Sign up for email news and select your interest groups at:
www.brfonline.org.uk/findoutmore/

Follow us on Twitter @brfonline

By post—to receive new title information by post (UK only), complete the form below and post to: BRF Mailing Lists, 15 The Chambers, Vineyard, Abingdon, Oxfordshire, OX14 3FE

Your Details
Name _____
Address_____
_____
Town/City _____ Post Code _____
Email_____

Your Interest Groups (*Please tick as appropriate)	
☐ Advent/Lent	☐ Messy Church
☐ Bible Reading & Study	☐ Pastoral
☐ Children's Books	☐ Prayer & Spirituality
☐ Discipleship	☐ Resources for Children's Church
☐ Leadership	☐ Resources for Schools

Support your local bookshop
Ask about their new title information schemes.